UNKNOWN
FRIENDS
WITHIN

PRAISE FOR

Unknown Friends Within

Unknown Friends Within is a powerful account of how one woman, Denise Grant, is navigating and making sense of her life. It is a story of how she is coming to know her alters and appreciate the valuable part they have played in helping her manage her early years of neglect, emotional and sexual abuse. This is not a finished story – it is still unfolding.

Throughout her account we come to know Denise, and her many alters, as complex, challenging, humorous and loving. It is an extraordinary read for anyone wishing to gain as insight into the lived experience of someone with Dissociative Identity Disorder. ~ *Laura Collister, Director, Mental Health, Research and Development, Wellways Australia*

This book is so rightly needed for those with DID. Denise is extraordinarily brave for revisiting this and letting the world into her world. *~Amanda Spedding, author*

I feel very privileged to have been able to read your extraordinary life story. It is an important and valuable lived experience that needs to be 'out there', informing and engaging a broad readership including anyone who is dealing with or has been touched by mental health issues as well as the doctors and therapists who try to help them and also the general public who want to learn more about the complexities of the human experience. *~Belinda Hulstrom, hypnotherapist*

Informative and entertaining! *~Christina R.*

A unique description of what it's like to live with DID and to have survived the traumas that produced your alters in the first place. *~Linda Black, hypnotherapist.*

An invaluable resource for those affected by DID.
~Julie Postance, author

For more than 50-plus years we have remained true friends with Denise, in a long-time friendship that has developed through many facets of our lives and as a result, we have a mutual bond built on love, loyalty, respect, and trust that can never be broken.

To watch a friend who you care for so deeply, go through such inner turmoil of mental anguish, depression and violent headaches mixed with periods of normality had at times been a roller coaster of emotions and as a result, we became good listeners and offered her support in any way possible.

We often found ourselves so confused about the way she behaved, changing before our very eyes, time and time again, all within an hour or so. Other times though, she was just Denise.

When Denise decided to seek out professional help and was eventually diagnosed with Disassociated Identity Disorder, there was a sense of relief and deep sadness within us as we tried to comprehend what she was going through. Through many long hours of discussions with Denise we were able to learn more about DID, which further strengthened our profound friendship.

We acknowledge and admire the courage and determination it took for Denise to write this book, and now she has finally achieved her goal of having her story published. Knowing this very exceptional lady as we do, there is no doubt in our minds that the road ahead will be surely full of many twists, turns and adventures. *~Carmel and Ray, friends of Denise*

Published in Australia by
Dilly Dally Books
PO Box 256, Doreen VIC 3754
denisegrant484@gmail.com
www.denisegrantsbook.com

First published in Australia 2021
Copyright © Denise Grant 2021

National Library of Australia Cataloguing in Publication entry

A catalogue record for this book is available from the National Library of Australia

ISBN: 978-0-6486979-0-9 (paperback)

Cover design by ICHD Designs.
Interior layout and design by Sophie White Design.
Printed by Ingram Spark

Unknown Friends Within

A Woman's Journey With Dissociative Identity Disorder

DENISE GRANT

CONTENTS

We need to stop
just pulling people
out of the river.

We need to go
upstream and *find
out why they're
falling in*.

~Desmond Tutu

FOREWORD

Denise was referred to me for marriage counselling almost 20 years ago, and never did either of us believe we would be here today. As a young psychologist in a suburban practice, I was used to dealing with run-of-the-mill issues, and it was not uncommon for a GP to refer clients to me as a last stop help for struggling couples. However, it was clear from the first session that the marriage was indeed over, Denise had reached a tipping point and asked to continue to see me to work through what that meant for her.

From my perspective, it was over the next 3-6 months that I started to see a pattern of behaviours both in the room as well as described to me that were not consistent with simply being depressed. When Denise started to talk about instances in the past that were particularly painful, a noticeable physical change would occur and, depending on the topic often her voice, body language, posture, composure, speech patterns and maturity would change in front of me. And then just as quickly Denise would be back, a little confused and usually diffusing the situation with a joke, but clearly confused about what had just happened. Over a period of months, I noticed that this would happen more and more, and it was as if the 'others' gained confidence and trust in me and allowed me to see more of them.

For me, I challenged myself and my thinking over those next few months – DID is exceedingly rare, was I really seeing it in front of me, how do I be sure it is DID? I certainly didn't want to use any therapeutic treatments that would risk planting false memories or confuse the diagnoses.

I consulted with senior peers, researched, and it became clearer that Denise was depressed, did have regular migraines, but also could be diagnosed with Dissociative Identity Disorder (DID).

But then to break the news to her, and the others, was something that took quite a bit of thought and planning – how do I make sure she/they can handle the news, ensure she had built up some resilience and support networks over the time, and also make sure that her children were available over the next week to help her process the news. Surprisingly or not surprisingly, I think that day was more a relief to her, her family, the others, and everyone around her and thus began the journey of more transparency, and an openness to get to know them better.

Some psychologists and psychiatrists recommend merging the personalities together over time as a treatment approach – this was never an option with Denise, as she nor I saw them as parts to be merged but rather as discrete and unique personalities that sought to be heard and understood, and even the most troublesome (yes Mizzy!) were well behaved and let Denise take the lead if they felt heard and understood.

-AR, psychologist

PART ONE

The Story

Until I was diagnosed with Dissociative Identity Disorder (DID) at the age of 50, I lived my life thinking I was much the same as everyone else. I did not consider that having multiple personalities was a point of difference.

This is my story of discovery, and how, with the help of my 12 alters – my multiple personalities – I survived extreme childhood neglect, debilitating loneliness, and sexual and emotional abuse.

My intention for sharing this story is to shed light on this complex and relatively unknown disorder. DID was not fully recognised until the late 1980s and many people have been misdiagnosed, as I was, living with the torment and confusion without appropriate support. It is my hope that through reading this book, other people with DID will find comfort and people without the condition can understand it better.

As with anyone living with mental health issues, people with DID can be fully functioning contributors to society. I personally have lived a fulfilling and adventurous life holding a variety of successful positions, marrying twice and have two wonderful children. I consider myself one of the luckiest people alive because of my DID. My alters have protected me from painful experiences because *they* carried the burden; *they* alleviated my suffering.

My story also challenges the longstanding stigma surrounding mental health issues and I believe that each lived experience shared, weakens its grip. It is still considered very normal to seek help for physical illness, however, those suffering mental ailments struggle to find appropriate support without judgement. Mental health expert Patrick Corrigan once said, "As humans, we all live under the same umbrella, but we travel down the river in different coloured boats." People with DID are simply sailing along in different coloured boats, quite possibly multi-coloured!

My son once asked me, "Mum, don't you feel like you've been cheated out of a life?"

My answer was a clear *no*. I've never known anything different. This was and is my uniquely beautiful life. To clarify, this story is my personal, lived experience of DID and mine alone. It may not represent your version of the same condition, nor is it intended to be a guide or self-help book for people with DID. I strongly encourage anyone suffering from the symptoms mentioned in this book to seek professional advice.

You may be more familiar with the term Multiple Personality Disorder, which is originally what the condition was called. An understanding of this rare and complex psychological disorder has evolved over time, which in basic terms refers to when a person's identity is fragmented into two or more distinct personality states called 'alters'. The 'splitting' is thought to be caused by a number of factors, the most prominent being severe physical, sexual and/or emotional trauma that usually occurred during childhood and was of an extreme, repetitive nature.

In my case, I developed DID as a result of childhood neglect, grief after the loss of my father, and sexual assault, all at a very young age. When I became overwhelmed from these events, I would dissociate or another personality would develop. Dissociating is an act of self-preservation; a way to manage and compartmentalise traumatic experiences.

When I was finally diagnosed with DID, I was gobsmacked to find that I had developed 12 different personalities, each one emerging at different stages of my life to help me cope with a variety of experiences. A common side effect of DID is loss of time, which I had also repeatedly experienced. Memory loss or a sense of having lost time occurs when an alter withholds the traumatic experience and its associated memories from you, to protect you from having to relive them. Often bearing the weight of disturbing memories is the reason a person might dissociate in the first place and birth an alter into existence.

Once dissociation occurs, the brain anchors it as a responsive mechanism to trauma. Thereafter, new alters are automatically created as needed. In some instances, certain alters may not reveal themselves and the memories they hold until much later down the track – possibly years. On some occasions they might reveal themselves but not the memories. In this way, living with alters and getting to know them is not a straightforward process in the slightest!

The reality is that living with DID is not easy. The challenges of losing time and memories, switching between identities, and being unexpectedly triggered to revisit past trauma, makes functioning in society as a person with DID to prove difficult at times.

I could describe the entirety of my life as a rollercoaster ride, dotted with thrilling episodes and jarring lows. Learning to manage my alters is a never-ending process and as there is no cure for my condition, I must pace myself to avoid all kinds of outcomes, some of which I will share with you in this book.

DID is a trauma-related disorder requiring self-care, compassion and professional support. It is not an illness a person is born with but it is life-long after its onset. Trauma counselling can help and in some instances it is suggested that the personalities are integrated. But for that to occur effectively the various alters need to be brought together so the individual becomes 'whole'.

Personally, I cannot, nor want to, consider that outcome. I love my alters. I love them for who they are and what they have been through. They all bare the mark of trauma and have not just survived but have protected me in the process. I have so much to thank them for and they are all a cherished part of me.

So, what does life look like for me and my alters?

Well, on a positive note, I can handle stress extremely well and tend to find myself in stressful situations quite often. I tend to *minimise* things perhaps a little too much, which enables me to work through stress in a detached manner. However, it is after the event – the debriefing stage between me and my alters – that's when things can become slightly unhinged!

You see, I am not the only one who has an opinion. It is

not just I who needs to contemplate an event, it is me and all my alters! And they all, or at least some of them, require time to think about it and express their process around this – it can be thoroughly exhausting!

Where some people might turn to drugs and alcohol to escape the ramifications of trauma, my alters step in to run the show. Where people turn to suicide as way out of a nightmare existence, my alters take the lead in a more life-affirming direction. Acts of self-sabotage one might choose as coping tools or a way to soften the hard edges of reality, again, I consider myself lucky for having developed the means to *dissociate,* for I could have taken many other troubled roads as a response to trauma. By the grace of God, I have been saved of those stories and instead, leaned into my alters, whether I had a say in it or not.

This is *our* story.

Introducing the Alters

As with anyone suffering from mental health issues, I have good and bad days.

Occasionally the bad days morph into months. It is *episodic.* Yet I receive amazing support from my family, friends, GP, psychologist, and psychiatrist. I choose continued care from these medical professions and have not felt forced to do so. The support network I have built enables me to live a healthy and enjoyable life despite the challenges I face with DID.

'So no more procrastinating! We will make a start on this book and see where it goes. Is that alright with you?' I announced to my guys.

(Mumble, mumble, mumble. More mumbles.)

'The time has come!' The Walrus says. 'To talk of many things.' [1]

And so, my friends have we! I say to my team.

Allow me to introduce you to my alters, whom I sometimes refer to as my alter egos or my guys. In doing so, it is my hope that people from all walks of life, and in particular, from within the mental health profession, find their contribution to this story as a means for improved understanding of Dissociative Identity Disorder. They each bring their own charisma, personal memories and set of circumstances to the broad and complex narrative that is my life and how I have learned to navigate and respond to childhood trauma.

---

1   From Lewis Carroll's *Through the Looking Glass and What Alice Found There, 1872*

Isobella	The little girl within. About nine years old.
Poppet	A little girl who was devastated by the death of my father. About 10–12 years old.
Mizzy	A teenager. Trying so hard to fit in. In her low-teens.
Quassie	He took the abuse 'on the chin' from my mother. Appears to be older than me.
Sassy One	Entangled in the sexual abuse while trying to find love. She has evolved with me.
Marm	Feels like we were judged by appearances. Needs things to be perfect. Older than me.
Jon	The gatekeeper for the other personalities. Now retired and enjoys gardening.
Logical One	Believes that if we were organised, all is fine. Age is undefined but has remained the same.
Spiritual One	The gentle soul who convinces me that all will be well; the yin to the yang of the Logical One.
Bob	He is fascinated with the universe. Ageless.
Janice	The angry one in the group who doesn't suffer fools lightly.
Old Man	A transient alter who held my hand when life was terribly confusing during the time I learned about my alters.
My Nothingness	More like a place I often found myself in when things became too overwhelming. One of the other alters would have filled this void for me but I may never know what happened.

I am usually aware of my 'switching' between the alters and it is so subtle that no one really notices except me. There are other times when I lose time completely. This is when an alter has taken over for whatever reason they have to do so.

So when I first started writing this book I was naïve to think that it was all about me – not so!

For it has never just been about me, it's been about me and my life with my alters. Since we will be telling this story together, I feel an introduction is in order of 'my team' as I sometimes refer to them. This will help guide you through the narration since they are going to have their input. For clarity's sake, I shall introduce them more in-depth in the same chronological order that they came to me, as listed above.

♦

Meet Isobella, the youngest of them all...

We all might have imaginary friends, or so we are told, but I don't think this is the case with her. I had always referred to her as Little Girl, as in, *the little girl within.* She originates from a time of loneliness, only comforted when my father was home. When he died, time stood still for Isobella. It appears she may have been forgotten entirely. However, this was corrected much later when she revealed herself more fully to me. That is how Isobella came to be my friend.

'You were so very lonely, weren't you?' she stated.

"Yes, but I didn't realise it at the time, Isobella. I had never known any other way except when my father was with me," I replied.

When I ponder the past, I feel Isobella was with me much of the time, making daisy chains, playing in rock pools and was ever so much more innocent and joyful. Even though she is about 9 or 10 years old, some of her memories date that further back.

Isobella is occasionally looked after by Marm and Jon, especially when events around her are beyond her comprehension or when things occur that a young girl need not to have to worry about. They gently remove her from those situations, which explains why I often find myself sitting down to a lunch of fairy bread or sandwiches filled with crisps or a plate of thinly sliced oranges coated in sugar.

Good one, Marm! Jon also encourages her to dig in the dirt. We certainly do have a colourful mixture of plants growing in the garden now.

(No landscape specialist needed here. I can hear a little titter from Mizzy.)

Jon also helps Isobella nurture a love of animals, hence, all the stuffed ones that share our humble abode. They are everywhere, the latest addition being a cute and fluffy, lop-eared rabbit called Willow the Wabbit.

Poppet also emerged after my father died, born into a world of pain and chaos. '*I didn't know what had happened and I didn't know what I was supposed to do. Nothing seemed real and no one spoke to me of what had happened.*'

I hear her on the verge of tears as she shares this with me, and I don't quite know what to say to her as I do not have a recollection of the time at all. My sense is that it was so painful, that all I recall is wanting to die as well. (I have since been told that this was likened to a catatonic state I entered since I have no memory of the time my father passed away.)

Poppet appears to remain as 11 to 12 years old and is dearly loved by us all. She is the fearful one though and whenever I feel unsure about something, it is her anxiety that consumes me. Again, I have Marm and Jon to thank, as they provide her with comfort in the form of cuddles and gestures of care.

Next in line is dear Quassie, a gentle soul but to look at him you wouldn't think so. He appears as a worn and battered fighter. He is short in stature, stooped over and covered in black and blue bruises. Quassie was always there when my mother told me off. On many occasions it was Poppet and I who could never do the right thing by my mother; we were always messing things up. Quassie, a little older and wiser, always seemed to be on duty. I don't know what we would have done without him, alongside Janice, who joined the team a little later.

Hold onto your hats! It's time to meet Mizzy! My goodness, she is your typical teenager, always up to mischief and sometimes quite rebellious. Mizzy remains a teenager but has always had the disposition to see the funny side in almost everything. And in sobering circumstances where there is no funny side, Mizzy takes great delight in messing with me, at times, making me appear to be an idiot saying inappropriate things at inappropriate times. Look out for Mizzy, who is possibly the loudest of the team. I know deep down she doesn't mean to be so troublesome.

'Don't I?' she giggled.

We have a great relationship even though she may seem a little cocky. Mizzy is the one who missed out on so much but now has the family she longed for. You see, much of my teenage life is blank to me. This must have been a lonely time for her. Nowadays, she is loved and cherished by us all – at the very least tolerated! (Said with tongue-in-cheek.) The alters seem to turn a blind-eye to some of her antics.

Even though Mizzy embarrasses me on occasion, I often hear Poppet having a giggle to herself; they seem to be good for each other. Mizzy will often say or do something funny, and I hear her belly-laughing in the background, with Poppet trying to hold back a snigger. All the while, I'm trying to fumble my way out of yet another real-time, awkward situation. Go figure!

Sassy One is possibly the most complex of the alters for she has never had any control over her own life. Always looking for someone to love us all, and, even when we did receive attention of a non-loving nature, she'd still take it. She could never say no. After all, it was her stepfather who told her it was *all her fault*. When having sex with some men, it didn't seem to be an issue if it wasn't really what she wanted. She always felt it was what she was *supposed* to do, or they wouldn't like her.

Even though Sassy One felt so ashamed of her sexual behaviour, her rationale was based on the importance of being noticed. I do believe my own self-worth issues emerged from here and still to this day, I struggle to resolve them.

This issue also became problematic between Sassy One and Mizzy. Even though Mizzy had her own rebellious streak, she was perplexed by Sassy One's choices. Yet Sassy One always struggled to differentiate between 'right and wrong' in these circumstances; it was all so perplexing for her.

Mizzy would say: *'Nice girls don't do that. Nice girls wouldn't even think of such things!'* which further compounded Sassy One's sense of worthlessness.

Enter stage left, Logical One. The alter who believes the answer to everything is to be organised, despite seeing how impossible that is for the whole team! Logical One experiences moods of frustration, which I feel points to when I am being so hard on myself.

'It's a beautiful day, Denise. Get out there and do something, even hanging the washing out would be something or go for a walk. Do something!' she said emphatically.

I know she is right but I'm tired. My head hurts so much. I just want to go to bed and bury myself under the doona. Thank God for Spiritual One!

Spiritual One, like Logical One, is older than me and the pair seem to hold the yin and yang balance of the group. Spiritual One always attempts to help me through my darkest moments by encouraging me to look at myself differently.

'Things will always work out as they should,' she reassured me.

Then there is Jon – who I realised later – was the Gatekeeper of the alters. I have no idea how Jon survived as I myself now struggle to keep the mob under control – Jon did seem able to keep us all in line, eventually. He is similar in age to me and presents as a gentle Englishman. Jon is content now, working in the garden and has become an apiarist. He loves his bees and holds them in such awe. Jon has been with me on numerous occasions when we have given presentations on beekeeping to Probus, View, gardening clubs and many others. He is immensely passionate about them. In fact, he says all animals are his best friends.

Then there is Bob, a very clever chap who never had the chance to prove himself at school despite his special interests in chemistry, physics and maths. (Interestingly, I excelled at these subjects in my youth and now I know why.) The universe and all that it encompasses is so vast and I have witnessed many discussions between Jon and Spiritual One contemplating metaphysical themes. Often times, Jon will chime in. Heaven helps us if Professor Brian Cox appears on TV or radio. It's a challenge for us all to listen in stillness and silence, we get so excited! (Brian Cox is a Professor of Particle Physics. He believes the universe, including our Earth is a beautiful, fragile place, as do we. The team and me.)

Allow me to introduce Janice, characterised by having a hot temper. Janice adores us all but gets frustrated when others, myself included, don't take notice of her. She gets the urge to scream and yell at us and on several occasions, has done so regardless of any bystanders around us. Janice was the invisible one for many years and I feel that without Quassie's presence in the early days, Janice would have given a right good 'whippen' to anyone who had upset me.

And so, the family has evolved...

Marm has a place for everything, and everything should be in its place. I can hear the others even now.

Mizzy thinks it's a hoot. *'Who is she kidding?'*

Logical One agrees with Marm, *'Life would be so much easier if we just got organised.'*

'We don't have enough room for everything though, Marm,' taunted Mizzy.

♦

God, it gets thoroughly complicated. A bit like going to a party and being introduced to others yet at the same time hearing voices in my head talking amongst themselves.

'Get a load of what she is wearing,' said Mizzy.

'Don't be so rude,' warned Marm.

'*I know but couldn't she have worn something that was at least clean?*'

'*Enough! Behave yourselves!*' commanded Logical One.

'*Where is the food? I am so hungry,*' said Poppet.

'*You are always hungry,*' remarked Mizzy.

And on and on they go.

Again, my pounding headache, ever-present.

And I am reminded of a quote. The sum of my experience:

There they go!
I must hasten to follow,
For I am their Leader!

~Alexandre Auguste Ledru-Rollin,
French Revolution Leader

Introducing Me, Denise

I am twice married and mother of two children. Jodie, my daughter, and Corey, my son, are both from my first marriage. After 11 years that relationship dissolved, and I went on to re-marry a few years later. After my second marriage broke down, I started having weekly-to-fortnightly counselling sessions with a psychologist and was prescribed medication by my GP.

In 2001, Annabel, my psychologist, diagnosed me with Dissociative Identity Disorder (DID). This was a turning point on my path, and I have since become fully aware of each member on my team. There are currently 12 alters, each possessing their own unique identities, opinions, and agendas.

Upon first learning about my alters, I was spun into a whirlwind of turmoil and disbelief. I could no longer attend work and the whole situation felt like a dream from which I could never wake up. I felt the end was near, that I was never going anywhere again. Put simply, I was a mess!

The other diagnoses I had been given was as a teenager, which included both severe and (occasional) manic depression. Yet in hindsight, there was something else hiding, something I was never aware of. It did not become clear that I had DID until I was approaching 50 years of age. I feel I have bluffed my way through life, mixed-up and isolated. My experience of life was for it to always feel out of my control and, not knowing any better, I just rolled with it.

The telling of my own story here has been important for my own sense of understanding my journey but equally important as a means to educate a wider audience about DID and challenge misconceptions about mental health issues and trauma-related responses, in general.

My sense is that many people can relate to some of the symptoms associated with DID as there are commonalities across other mental health conditions, such as depression, panic attacks and anxiety disorders, and that knowing they are not alone in their experience is of real comfort.

I have also encountered psychologists and psychiatrists who have not yet come across DID until they met me. I hope my story serves to help correctly diagnose people with the condition by providing deeper insight into this complex condition. In many cases, mine included, people with DID are misdiagnosed from the outset, rendering the appropriate treatment delayed for many years.

I also want to reach out to young people who are suffering childhood trauma such as emotional neglect, sexual abuse, and mistreatment in its many forms, to highlight that none of it is acceptable and that their voice matters. They are deserved of care and support to protect them from the acts of perpetrators; that it never is nor ever was their fault to begin with. Thankfully, this is spoken about more freely now and I hope my book continues to open such dialogue.

Unknown Friends Within has been a long time coming. It has also been a challenge for me to pull it together. Making sense of all my journals to create a coherent narrative of my life has been overwhelming at times and then the task of integrating all my alters brings a whole other set of challenges in itself, but it has been well worth it.

'Just make a start, please!' begged Logical one.

'The garden has got to be done and soon, as it has been neglected of late,' Jon reminded me.

Do I do a full day in the garden and ignore everyone? Or do I attempt a small chunk each day and attend to some of the other's stories too?

'Pity there are so many of us,' said Mizzy, *'for there are only seven days in a week.'* She giggled as she added, *'and that would mean someone might miss out!'*

Despite her jokes, she might have a point, until I see Logical One drawing up a plan. *'If only we could get organised and work to a timetable, it may help overcome the chaos. Then everyone knows what is expected.'*

Spiritual One doesn't feel it's necessary to be so dogmatic. Like Mondays are for bed changing and tidy-ups between 8:00am–10:00am. Spiritual One is only too aware of how things just seem to happen.

♦

As my psychologist Annabel pointed out, I must get structured! I heard her words and thought I understood them but realised I could not quite grasp their meaning, which is made all the more challenging with multiple personalities running the show.

Once upon a time when I was blissfully unaware, I thought I had a structured life. I knew, or thought I knew, the events of the day ahead. There was routine, purpose. I dare say a sense of 'normality'. Little did I know then that I was merely obeying orders from my alters; that if my feelings, desires or dreams surfaced, they were quickly locked away and unacknowledged. They would have tipped the delicate balance that was dictated by my multiple personalities. I am grateful for Annabel's advice to pursue writing in my journal, which helped me put space between the many contributors and eventually formed the backbone of this story.

These days, more people are raising their hands to voice their true story of what it's like to live with a mental health condition and from that willingness to share we are breaking down stigma, isolation, and misconceptions. We have come a long way since I first developed my alters, a time when there was still so much to learn about this fascinating and self-preserving response to trauma.

In my eyes, I am one of the lucky ones. My survival technique was to dissociate and in doing so I have lived an adventurous, fulfilling, remarkably rich and rare kind of existence.

The First Discovery

'Oh! What a tangled web we weave.
When first we practice to deceive!'

~Sir Walter Scott

I have always loved my bed. On this particular morning, it was no different. I stretched out, revelling in taking my time to get up, when it suddenly became obvious that something was wrong. What exactly was it that struck me to sit up and through bleary eyes, look around my bedroom?

I struggled to fully waken and sharpen my focus but once I did, I could answer my own question. I realised I was still wearing my clothes from the night before. I was in the outfit I had worn to a function with some colleagues. I was, at the time, the Assistant Accountant and Office Manager, and we had been on a staff cruise up the Yarra River for dinner. I last recalled dancing with the Payroll Officer, Bev. Now I was in my own bed, in the same dinner clothes and it was 1:30pm the next day. What the hell had happened?

Panic set in as I ruminated over the lost time. My head was throbbing. I felt sick. Nothing was coming back to me, and I felt frightened. *Stop it! Pull yourself together!* I commanded. But what the bloody hell did I do?

I managed to get myself out of bed, have a shower and a cup of coffee and then *THINK!* But try as I might, I still could not recall anything. I had absolutely no memory of the previous night and as panic set in further, I struggled to breathe. Surely I couldn't have drunk that much? Tomorrow, being Monday, I would have to go to work. I would have to find out what happened then.

What will I say to everyone?

What did I do?

What will they all think of me?

In my state of confusion, I fumbled through Sunday only to find a sum of cash stashed away in my handbag. Where had it come from? At this point my headache was so bad, I was finding it hard to see. The light piercing through the curtains was blinding and I still felt sick. I had lost all sense of time. Again.

The next thing I knew, it was Monday morning and I was driving myself to work. I was driving along Ferntree Gully Road heading to Mulgrave. I passed some pylons in the middle of a cow paddock. It occurred to me it wouldn't take long to just do it! Then I found myself steering in their direction, headed straight for a pylon! It seemed like a swift solution and an end to my constant headaches, the confusion and panic, the ever-present knot in my stomach, all of which had been part of my life for so long. I quickly began to blank out. The next thing I knew I was atop a hill with no idea as to how I got there – it was Wheelers Hill. And another attempt at suicide, it appeared, and thank God, this one didn't work either.

Was this all a dream I could not wake from?

It dawned on me that I was headed for work in Mulgrave and I was going to have to face everyone, despite not knowing anything. God help me, if they said anything insulting or made me the laughingstock, I would just get in my car and drive home. I braced myself with the decision that I would never need to see or speak to them again.

I parked the car. I entered the building. I stepped into the unknown.

"Morning, Denise!"

"Great night on Saturday!"

"Hiya, Denise."

♦

What the hell?

I was greeted with warm salutations. Everyone seemed pleased to see me. So I went to my desk, completely flummoxed and a bit dazed. I made myself a coffee and got on with the day. As I entered the kitchen, I was greeted again.

"Here she is! Thanks for a great night, Denise."

Everyone chimed in with the same sentiments. There were smiles all round. I was embraced. I snatched a look at the cork notice board. There were new photos spread all over. One of which was me doing the limbo with my skirt pulled up and tucked into my knickers! Under that pole I went, laughing my head off. I was in disbelief. What had possessed me?

I motioned to one of my colleagues to join me outside. "Was I really that drunk?" I asked.

"You weren't drunk at all," she said. "In fact, I only remember seeing you with one drink all night."

"So what happened? I only remember dancing with Bev and then the next minute, I'm at home in bed."

I could tell she was reading grave concern across my face and made an effort to set the story straight. "My goodness, Denise, you really don't remember, do you? After we came back and left the cruise, you told us all to follow you. You took us to the Casino, taught us how to play Blackjack, won heaps of money yourself and bought everyone a round of drinks. It was great! We all want to go out with you again!"

None of this made any sense to me; I had no idea how to play Blackjack. "Bloody hell!" was all I could say. I found the relaying of events overwhelmingly confronting and made my way back to my desk, trying to wrap my head around it all, to no avail.

Meanwhile, my manager, Alec, had put the monthly reports on my desk, ready to be entered into the computer and reconciled. I was still frayed around the edges, thinking a quick fag, a fresh cup of coffee, then I'll get stuck into them.

I returned to my desk, calmer and clearer. The reports were nowhere to be seen! I had left the desk for all but 10 minutes. I scoped the open-plan office, thinking perhaps someone was playing a trick on me. Everyone sat heads-down studiously taking no notice of my paranoia. I quietly rummaged about my desk until I eventually found them. They were filed away, signed off by me. Job, done and dusted.

I was seeing my psychologist, Annabel, at the time and was due to catch up with her the following week, so I began to jot down a few notes documenting all these strange occurrences. The black outs, the loss of time, the Blackjack. I felt slight relief I could workshop these occurrences with her soon and until that time came around, I would try to remain calm. Unfortunately, the following Friday night, I was triggered into panic once again.

On this occasion, I had committed to babysitting for my sister, Kerrie, who lived in a suburb near the beach. I was on the long drive there, almost arrived, when I pulled up at a set of lights. It was one of those balmy, seaside evenings with the sun slowly setting. I sat gazing out the window, contemplating the beauty of a simple sunset when a cow caught my eye. *Having her last munch for the day*, I thought to myself. Everything seemed as it should be, and I recall an overarching tranquillity.

This turned on a dime.

I suddenly didn't recognize anything around me. I was in my car but no longer at the lights. No cow, no sunset. I seemed to be near a freeway elevated above me. How the hell did I arrive here? I checked the time. It was 8:15pm. Hell's bells, I was due at Kerrie's at 7.

'Turn around and go back the way you were coming. Maybe you will recognise something,' said a voice within.

I did as I was told and eventually reached Kerrie's, but she was furious that I was late. I attempted explaining it to her but even I was having trouble stringing the truth together. I had no idea what had just occurred, and it showed. It was now too late for her to go out, and so I left.

Again, the headache set it, the panic, knotted stomach. The onset took over and I was clutching for answers. I soothed myself with the knowledge of seeing Annabel next week when I would attempt to relay the blackouts. I was petrified there was something seriously wrong with me. I was worried I had lost my mind.

♦

"Am I going mad?" I asked Annabel.

"No," she smiled, "but I would like you to go back and see Dr Lee."

She handed me a note for him. I went home and made an appointment for the next day.

Dr Lee arranged for me to have a brain scan. The results confirmed that everything was fine but he advised me to continue seeing Annabel.

"What was wrong then? Why did you organise a brain scan?" I enquired.

"We just want to rule out the possibility of petit mal seizures – but all is fine."

'But I do have a brain, at least?' said Mizzy. (Unbeknownst to Dr Lee it was her questioning.)

"Most definitely!" he reassured with a smile.

◆

At my next consultation with Annabel I announced, "I am not having petit mal seizures." Although it hadn't occurred to me that at this stage, if I wasn't having seizures then what on Earth was wrong with me?

"Good," she said, "I just wanted to make sure."

"Okay! So now what?"

Annabel went on to tell me a story about a little girl whose father died when she was 10 years old and how her childhood had been extremely lonely. She explained that the girl was abused by her stepfather and later, by another man. At this point, I was crying my eyes out.

"What's wrong, Denise?" Annabel gently asked.

"Oh, Annabel, that is so sad!" As my tears poured forth, it dawned on me that the little girl Annabel was talking about, was me.

I was in shock as it slowly registered that those horrible

events had actually occurred to me. I rocked in my chair, biting my lip to distract me from the psychological pain of my past. It was March 2001 and I was 49 years old. For the first time in my life, I seem to be taking ownership of it and all that occurred in my childhood.

It was *my* father who died 39 years ago.

Not someone else's, *mine.* It was really my father and he had died. The pain I was now experiencing was unbearable. My head felt like it was going to split in two. I wanted to scream. Scream and yell. All I could do was cry and keep crying. I was still biting my lip, rocking back and forth.

And then I stopped.

I felt nothing, abruptly. I'm sitting very still, gazing out the window, when I heard Annabel ask if I was okay.

'No, I'm not,' a little voice replied. 'Why did my daddy die and where is he now?'

What?! Who is this little one?

It felt like I was eavesdropping, witnessing a dream.

'It wasn't nice, what David and Don did either, was it?' A different voice chimed in – whose voices was I now hearing?

Then a rush of sickness kicked in. *This* had really happened to me as well. Not this, please no! Not this!

I wasn't sure what to do with *this* so I just sat. I was playing with my necklace and continued staring out the window. The realization of what David had done to me landed upon my shoulders with such horrid truth that I felt physically sick and wanted to flee.

'But where would you run to, my dear?' It was Spiritual One, a different and older voice, gently probing me.

My goodness, who are you? I wondered. Surely, I was dreaming. These fragmented voices; could this be real?

Then as suddenly as this conversation started, it ended in a flash. I brought my awareness to the present moment. I was in Annabel's room again with necklace in hand. Subtle sounds emerged in the space around us. "Oh my God, Annabel! What is wrong with me?"

I wasn't expecting her to give me a straight answer and yet she did. Like a curve ball spun into my mind without warning, her diagnoses landed and I am shocked. I remember this single moment like it was yesterday.

It was an autumn day in March 2001 and Annabel said to me, "I believe you are suffering from Dissociative Identity Disorder. This is the new and acceptable name for Multiple Personalities."

♦

The only reference I had for understanding Multiple Personalities was from the movie, *Sybil*. Yet I am nothing like her. I'm not a homicidal killer, for goodness sake! I could not relate in the slightest. I was thinking: *You've got to be kidding me! No! Not me!* Things like this just didn't happen to people like me. I was a fully functioning adult.

As I grappled with all that led me to this point, I realised that my guys had been leading me through this maze of a life, guiding me to do whatever I needed to do to survive. And that now I had to surrender any notion of ever returning to that innocence; to the unawareness that I have Dissociative Identity Disorder. That from this point onwards it was a defining factor. Somewhere in the chaos of my mind (or was it now *our* mind?) I tried to salvage the thought that I would get over all this, that I would return to who I once was. It was a shock to face the truth that that reality was long-gone from existence.

So, what to do now?

'Well for starters, you can stop feeling sorry for yourself,' said Mizzy.

'But I don't Mizzy, I don't feel sorry for myself. It's just...'

'Just what?'

'Well, I guess it's just a little hard to fully grasp the meaning of it all.'

Here I pause, for the enormity of it hits me. I am lost for words.

♦

My inability to focus was frightening. I was so aware of the others, of how different their needs and perspectives of the world were. Yet in the past, it seemed okay. They each played a part. They knew the role they had to play and took centre stage when the curtain was raised. Sometimes they shared the limelight, other times they performed solo. I assumed some even withdrew backstage at times, unaware of one another and how each life scene connected to the next.

But now the play was over, and we were here! *All* centre stage, *all* face-to-face, for the very first time. I was amazed. My life, with a cast of so many, seemed over and now the future belonged to us all. Together we had to make sense of the real world *and* the DID world and leave the theatre for good. We are a motley crew with me in the middle, knowing I'm the one to make the decisions, *for I am their Leader,* yet I struggled with the decisions for they are also so aware, that *I am aware,* and everyone wants to be heard.

Even though I am aware of my personalities and can recognise who is present, I sometimes switch from one alter to another; so subtle is the change. Deeply do they hide at times, not even I can notice. And soon I learned that close family and friends could barely tell who had come to the surface. Hours ran into days, the days into weeks, and weeks rolled into months. I had no concept of time, just sort of wandered aimlessly. Or so I think, I don't remember.

I maintained contact with Annabel though, who admitted she had never worked with a client like me. We were both sailing unchartered waters and made the commitment that if either of us felt our relationship was not working, we would promptly seek outside help.

All the lies, all the pretence; the deeply hidden stories of my past. The memories all buried among my alters, they were given space *to breathe*. It was safe for them to be unearthed – it is quite a process. I was eager to move forward but was spinning in the middle, being pulled in all directions, by one and then another.

'Do this!'

'No, do that!'

'Why don't we start on sorting this out?'

Several voices chimed in at once.

OH, FOR A BIT OF PEACE AND QUIET!

My head hurt.

If only I could bring them all to order. How wonderful that would be. But I yearned to have the energy. Perhaps tomorrow.

♦

Annabel was knee-deep with investigations and chanced upon a scientist who was studying DID through a university in Hawthorn. She suggested we try and meet with the scientist, which I eagerly agreed to. Together we arranged to meet with Dr Joe.

He was a friendly chap and pleased to meet us. "I am working with a group of people who have been diagnosed with this condition and I have a group of actors working alongside them," he said, then went on to describe how he was monitoring the brain waves of both groups when they were given specific tasks or asked to think of a special event. "There is no doubting that there are differences between the groups. It appears that those with DID definitely have a smaller hippocampus," he declared.

"The hippocampus is a part of the brain," he went on. "It is found in the inner folds of the bottom middle section of the brain, known as the temporal lobe."

Good! Clear as mud, I thought, for I had very little idea about what he spoke of next.

He explained:
- Humans have known about the hippocampus for over four centuries. It is one of the most studied parts of the brain with its main functions involving human learning and memory. Knowing about the hippocampus has helped researchers understand how memory works.
- The hippocampus is important for learning and forming memory, and is part of the limbic system which is associated with the functions of feeling and reacting.
- These structures help control bodily functions such as the endocrine system and what is commonly known as the 'fight or flight' response.
- Smaller hippocampal volume has been reported in

several stress-related, psychiatric disorders including Post-Traumatic Stress Disorder, Borderline Personality Disorder where early abuse is apparent, as well as Depression.

• Patients with Borderline Personality Disorder paired with early abuse have smaller amygdala volume of the hippocampal and amygdala. Their volumes have been examined in individuals with DID, as this condition is associated with having a history of severe childhood trauma.

Dr Joe explained the methods of his research, which involved the use of magnetic resonance imaging applied to measure the volumes of the hippocampus and amygdala. Among 15 male and 23 female, all with DID or other psychiatric disorders, the volumetric measurements for the groups were compared. The results: hippocampal volume was 19.2% smaller and amygdala volume was 31.6% smaller in the individuals with DID compared to individuals without. The ratio of hippocampal volume to amygdala volume was significantly different between groups. In conclusion, the findings were consistent with the presence of smaller hippocampal and amygdala volumes in patients with DID compared with individuals who did not have the condition.

So there you have it. It appeared my hippocampus is small. This all made perfect sense and I hoped like hell that Annabel was taking notes so that she could explain his findings to me in plain English!

Although I did enquire with Dr Joe about my constant headaches and their severity, to which he explained that these were caused by the different neurological changes in my brain when I switched between alters, whether it be during slight nuance of change or when I experienced significant time loss. Other symptoms of DID he had noticed were amnesia, trances and 'out of body' experiences.

"If you dissociate, you may feel disconnected from yourself and the world around you. Dissociation is one way the mind copes with too much stress, such as during a traumatic event," he explained.

Yep! A few more boxes ticked, and I was on my way to understanding the conversation about DID a little more easily. It was true. I am, at times, completely unaware of my body whereby it seems like I am in a trance. Perhaps all these neurological changes could be the reason I got so tired. We thanked Dr Joe for his input to our investigations, of which I took on board.

It was as though, up until now, my life had been shared with others. My alters would come and go as *they* saw fit, and I had no idea how to take control. I suppose a lot of the time, I did not have much of my own voice to share either, so I allowed them to take the reins. Taking over here, taking over there. Me, always in a spin, wrestling with confusion. I stood in the middle of this whirlwind, and they would run amok! No, *I* have never been confused, they just pulled me in so many different directions with conflicting opinions, each with their own agendas playing out in my life.

My memories are like a dream. Fragmented. Recalling bits here and there. Remembering events in parts, never with cohesion. Annabel tried to liken it to playing tag-team. *'Tag, you're it!'* And it was. My memories are intermingled with the memories of my alters rendering such difficulty, all my life, in searching for clear answers. To find a semblance of peace has been near impossible. Until I reached a salient point, a shift in my perspective. I reframed, ever so slightly, to reach a level of meaning. An acceptance I must hold on to.

For it has never been *just* my life.

♦

Over the coming months I signed up for the adventure of 'formally' meeting my *Unknown Friends Within*. It was in the company of Annabel – who was asking to speak to each one individually – as well as during my journal writings, that they began to emerge and introduce themselves.

Little Girl was the first to appear. Lonely and timid, so frightened was her manner. She didn't really know what was going on and had been lost in time since her father passed away. She later identified herself as Isobella.

Poppet, who was about 11 years old now, explained it was she who recovered from the catatonic state I had been in that had been triggered by the awful pain I could not bear after my father passed away. Now, she felt totally unprepared for life itself. Nothing made any sense to her. So much changed and it was left up to her to deal with it. Bewildered and overwhelmed as to how to become part of this new life she found herself in, was extremely tough for young Poppet. The burdens she carried thus spilled into the grief she caused for her mother. She was aged 10 when Quassie had to step in.

Quassie (short for Quasimodo) appeared to me as a man of short stature, with bumps and bruises presenting all over his misshapen physique. Quassie certainly took it for our team, for he was the one who felt the depth of my mother's anger and frustration. Her wrath.

The Teenager, the rebellious one, made her presence known. She challenged Annabel on many occasions from the outset, displaying typical teenage angst. She loathed being a 'loser', victimised by events happening around her and never really understood The Why. I liken The Teenager to a rabbit caught in headlights with her propensity to be on the defence, then misbehave.

Sassy One was from a different kettle of fish altogether. Riddled with guilt and shame, she found it exceedingly difficult to associate with the others.

A usual day with the likes of this motley crew ranged from drama to mixed emotion:

Teenager's face spoke a thousand words. She was mortified. *'What the hell?'*

Sassy One wanted to crawl away in shame. *'I am so sorry. All I wanted to do was find someone to love me.'*

Then Poppet jumped in. *'There was never anyone who was there to guide her. I feel sorry for her.'*

And so it came about, that not only did *I* not know of all of them to begin with but there were also alters who were unaware of each other. Teenager required time to process the current circumstances.

'Leave her be,' Marm said. *'I will look after her.'*

"And who might you be?" I tentatively asked.

'Just call me Marm.'

♦

Her voice was calm and reassuring with a hint of authority. I had better watch out for this one.

It was around this time when each alter began revealing

themselves that I asked Annabel as to why this had all happened. How did I not know of them before? She reasoned that it was because of an alter referred to as The Gatekeeper – the one that held the order – who simply could not cope anymore and allowed for this process to occur.

"Do you remember the week prior to you becoming aware of lost time, Denise?" she enquired. "I think so much happened and unlike other times when you were under stress and able to minimise everything, I think that this time was all too much for The Gatekeeper. He gave up."

That really was the time that everything turned on a dime.

I was grateful I had Annabel by my side, for what ensued was the separation from my then husband, Col, and I was to move into a new home. Corey, my son, was leaving for England and I had no idea when I would see him again. At the same time, a dear friend unexpectedly moved interstate. I crumbled, horrendously. I did not know what to do. So I turned to Annabel.

She looked at me squarely. "For goodness sake, Denise. Don't you realise that for most people these sorts of struggles occur over a period of months to years and they would have a hard time coping. You have gone through all of this in one week. No wonder you are feeling lost. It's a lot to deal with."

"I guess." I shrugged, not totally convinced. It was all getting a bit unbelievable. I couldn't comprehend how this was happening.

Then Annabel caught me off guard with her next question. "Why don't we ask them?"

"My goodness, you've got to be joking?!"

She smiled. "Just close your eyes and see what happens."

And so I did. I sat and I continued sitting. Nothing

occurred. I was about to open my eyes when a gentlemen presented before me.

'I am deeply sorry, Denise. I did try but with so many twists and turns, I just did not know what to do anymore. They have been a bit of a handful for a long time and now I have become so tired.'

♦

I was on a mission now to try and understand my life. Tiredness was all consuming. I wondered if it might ever end but I persevered regardless, to get to know all sides of the story within me; of these *Unknown Friends Within* me, who had journeyed my life alongside me for so long and down so many forgotten paths.

How to attribute them all? To ensure they would all be heard. I took to my journals with ruthless dedication, allowing them all the space to speak through me. Affording them the freedom to simply *be*. Often times muddled, they all had something to say, jumping in, unprompted. Uninhibited.

I had opened Pandora's Box. I unravelled the tangled web. Inside there was a story, *my* story, with many different beginnings and many different endings. Of joy and sadness entwined. It would be as much *our* story as it was mine and I was committed to seeing it through, but first some key instructions from the crew:

The Teenager's name is Missy.

'No, not Missy!' She corrected. 'It's Mizzy, spelt with a double z. Not s.'

Marm wanted me to emphasise that if it weren't for her, we would never have 'Kept Up Appearances'. I knew she was struggling with my lack of attention, having so many things on my mind. I could barely keep up with the housework let alone the conversations running inside me.

'I have learnt to be patient though,' she said *'But don't think I have given up. You will do your chores before too long, I hope! In the meantime, I will help with the little ones as we all struggle to make sense of all this. Maybe Jon can help me.'*

"And who might Jon be?" I asked for clarification.

'I am Jon.' He was the same man who had appeared in Annabel's room looking weary and a tad despondent. Again, he apologised. I attempted to tell him it was fine but I did enquire as to what I was supposed to do now?

'Mmmmm. A bit of a tough one,' he answered. *'They are your problem now. You will find your way, though.'*

I later learned that Jon was a gardener, so I genuinely wanted to do more of this. He, along with Isobella, loved all the animals I had gathered and would take time-out to watch the rabbits, the lovebirds, the chickens and Beau.

'A bit like retirement,' Mizzy retorted.

'Shut up, Mizzy, he has had a breakdown and deserves time-out,' Janice insisted.

Jodie found it hysterical that only one part of you can have a breakdown.

Surprise, surprise. I was introduced to two more: Logical One and Spiritual One. Despite much love between the two, they saw things very differently. Both are about the same age; a little older than me, perhaps. Logical One seemed to side with Marm, I had noticed, and it was her passion to be organised. It was her I needed to thank for all the notes I found about my home. A list for this, a list for that and the occasional one that said: Sort Out Lists.

Spiritual One would soften the edges, reminding me that, *'It was fine to have lists but take some time out for yourself also, my dear.'*

And so the journey had begun. Despite my mother insisting, "Just tell them to go away, they are making you physically ill. Put them back in the box and get on with your life", I carried on in pursuit of the truth, on my path of ultimate discovery.

And so I present to you, in as clear and cohesive fashion as my Dissociative Identity Disorder enables, the heart and soul of the story of how my alters came to be and the colourful life that ensued in their profound and precious company.

PART TWO

My Story

I was conceived out of wedlock, at which time it was not regarded in the same acceptable light as it is now. Back in those days, no one spoke of it. It just happened. My parents later married in England, and I have since learned that my mother did try to abort me on numerous occasions. This itself can be harmful to a baby. She was unsuccessful and I was born in Warwick, England in 1951.

My father, a Petty Officer with the Australian Navy as well as being an industrial chemist, wanted me to be raised in Australia, so when I was 11 months old we sailed across the seas to the Great Southern Land. The day we left was described by Nana Mab (my mother's mother) as one of the saddest days of her life. I was her first grandchild, and she was also my godmother. She adored me and was utterly miserable over the fact she may never see me again. Australia was a long way away, back then.

This was a difficult time for my mother too. I sensed some resentment from her which may have been partly due to the move, that essentially was being made for me. I only remember snippets of my childhood within which my mother never featured strongly. After arriving in Australia, we moved around at first until settling down with my grandparents, Nana and Grandad Perkins (my father's mum and dad). They lived in Merlynston in the northern suburbs of Melbourne. How long we lived with them, I do not know. This Nana used to call me Chicken.

Next, we moved into a house in Hampton, a small abode that belonged to someone else. I recall playing dress-ups with another little girl in some gowns that belonged to her mother. We draped jewellery on ourselves, loads of beads, and strutted around in high-heels. Even though I can't quite picture the dresses, I clearly remember how they felt. They were exquisitely soft.

I also have this vague memory of another man's house. I'm unsure as to whether we lived there or if we just visited but he had a lidded jar of periwinkles hidden away in a cabinet. I still vividly remember the smell that came from the jar when the lid was removed – like the smell of ocean air.

My first *real* home was an old, rather large, two-storey house with an outside bathroom and toilet. My father used to light a fire in the heater above the bath with kindling about an hour before we could have hot water.

The house itself was across the road from the beach, on the corner of Beach Road and Genoa Street in Mentone. I was five years old when we started living there. Ron and Nola Oswald lived in Genoa Street too and they soon became friends with my parents. They had a son, David, who was 14 months younger than me and I recall Uncle Ron saying that David and I would one day get married. He wanted a daughter but for reasons I did not understand at the time, they couldn't have one.

I would follow along with my father and Uncle Ron to gather mussels off the rocks near the old pier. It was safe to do this back then as pollution was a concept barely in existence. When our hessian bags were full to the brim, home we would go and boil them up in a big old copper. I am yet to taste better mussels to this very day.

On the odd Sunday we would pick up a chicken or two from the poultry farm, bringing them home still alive. I would watch in horror as my father and Uncle Ron would sharpen the axe. I knew what was coming next and would cover my eyes. I could hear David yelling, "You gotta look at this! Don't be such a sissy!" and as I buckled under his command I'd see a poor chicken running headless. David thought it was funny and would chase it.

I didn't like it in the slightest but pretended to laugh to appease him so he didn't think I was silly. This one occasion was the only time I watched, and Isobella wanted to cry, *'Poor Chicken!'* We were given its feet to play with once they'd been separated from the body. If you pulled at the gristle, the feet would open and close. I found that part to be fun.

I also recall the smell in the outside laundry where the chickens were plucked. Wet feathers were strewn everywhere and the smell was putrid. One day David, along with his mate from down the street, Kevin, decided we should all play a game of hide and seek. They put me in a steamer trunk so that I couldn't see where they were hiding. It seemed fine until I heard the clasps on the lid shut tight. I called out but no one answered. Yelling and screaming and crying, I was awfully frightened. *I'm going to die!* I thought. Then everything went blank.

The next thing I recall was someone pulling me out and my mummy standing in front of me. I wanted her to hug me, to reassure me, but she didn't. Instead, she walked off saying I was being silly and to be careful when playing with the boys. I felt incredibly alone and blanked out again. Now I realise that Isobella had been with me throughout this experience, and it was she who had dealt with my fear and the rejection from my mother while I remained blanked out. Thank you, Isobella.

My childhood is dotted with fond memories that while they seem less significant to me now, I know they are cherished by Isobella. Like the Guy Fawkes nights when we'd pile wheelbarrows high for the burn, gazing at the sky, firecrackers lighting up the starry night.

It was an exciting time for the entire neighbourhood. All the fathers and the older boys made convoys of wheelbarrows filled with the rubbish we had been collectively saving during the year. Across to the cliffs they would go and pile the contents high. Old rubber tyres, paint tins, wood, unwanted clothing, old bikes, toys, anything that nobody needed. It didn't matter what it was. If it could burn, then it was all piled up so, so high.

This was always a special night, and each year we challenged ourselves to build the biggest and the best bonfire for miles. There were many bonfires dotted along the cliffs of the bay but we would all agree: we had done it. Ours was the best.

Then the crowning glory – Guy Fawkes – all dressed up in his finery of old discarded clothes stuffed with anything and everything including straw and paper, would take his place high on top of the bonfire. There he would stand tall and proud until the darkness emerged, and we would all gather with our fireworks and thermos full of hot chocolate waiting for the signal to go out.

It was time! The bonfire would be set alight and firecrackers would fire up the night sky, along with the most deafening noises of the penny bungers and cartwheels, intermingled with everyone's voices.

"Oooh!"

"Ahh, look at that one!"

"Oh, did you see that one?"

They truly were the most wonderful nights, etched in my memory all this time.

On one other special night, I was taken outside and my father lifted me up onto his shoulders and insisted, "Watch and keep watching!" As I did, a brightly lit shape flashed across the black sky. "Did you see it?" he asked.

"Yes, Daddy, I did. What was it?"

"It was the Sputnik!" he announced.[2]

This sense of adventure my father ignited was what lit Isobella and me up, softening the shadow of loneliness that was cast upon our childhood.

There were many adventures such as visiting the old coal shed, the Rawlings man and his little van and the simple joy of hanging out the washing with my mother, to include our doll's clothes pegged across the line. There was daisy picking with David to weave daisy chains and of course, the day my first sister, Myra was born – she was a sickly child, her room

---

2   Sputnik was the first artificial Earth satellite launched by the Soviet Union on October 4th 1957. Sputnik orbited for three week before its batteries died, then circled the planet silently for two more weeks before falling back into the atmosphere.

always smelling of medicines. Then two and a half years later, arrived baby Kerrie.

But most importantly was Mr Harry's corner store, one of our favourite places to visit. I'll never forget the comforting sound when a bell used to ring over the shop door whenever anyone arrived, and the step up at the entrance was wooden and well-worn, even back then.

We loved visiting as it was a bit of an Aladdin's Cave; wooden shelves with an assortment of everyday items and aisles with similar goods, old jars and boxes making it an extremely exciting place for a young girl. I would hover around the counter and stand on tippy toes so that Mr Harry could see me.

"Are there any broken biscuits today Mr Harry?" I would sheepishly ask.

"Well, I don't know," he would say while reaching for one of the old biscuit tins. (I think he always knew there would be some but he always made me wait.) Down came a tin and as he lifted the lid back, he would be pull out a brown paper bag too. "Well look at that," he would say. "I think there are some at the bottom here!"

"Thank you!" I would say but I couldn't wait until I was outside to see what was in the brown bag. If I was lucky, there would be broken chocolate biscuits – these were my favourites. I made sure I ate them on my way home and the rest I would give to my mother who would make brownies with them. I often find myself wondering well into my adult years, whatever became of Mr Harry and his little corner grocery shop.

During these years, my mother was henceforth preoccupied with her younger children, which I suppose was the natural order. My father was different, however. He strongly figures as a special person in my life. The memories I hold dearest and clearest are with him. Whenever he was home, my life felt good.

I started school when I was six, commencing in first grade. It was a long, lonely trek by myself to the bus stop where I would catch the bus that would then drop me off near the school entrance At school, it seemed another chance of making friendships diminished as many children already knew each other from kindergarten, of which I never attended. I didn't have birthday parties. I didn't have many friends. I think I attended only one party at which my mother made me wear a bright green dress with a bib. The straps met the bib with black buttons. I was so embarrassed. We grew used to being alone, Isobella and me. My favourite game was to play in rock pools with the seaweed wrapped around my legs. I was a mermaid and we spent long stretches of time swishing my tail in flow with the currents of the water. I would sing, "I'm a little mermaid," and in that moment, I was.

My parents had been saving for a new house and it was with much excitement that we eventually moved into our new home in Mentone. I was about eight by then and I even had a bedroom to myself, and we had an indoor bathroom and toilet. It was extremely exciting. Our house was one of the first to be built in a new estate. It was a modern brick veneer with three bedrooms, Daddy didn't even have to stoke up the old wood heater so we could have hot water. Not like the old house in Mentone.

No! This was luxury! Running hot water whenever we wanted it.

I didn't understand and, to be honest, I still to this day do not understand why my mother thought it would be a good idea to have a burgundy-coloured bathtub, wash basin and toilet but the fact that it was all indoors made it great nevertheless. We had instant heat and no fire heater above it. The colour was unimportant to me, but I still wonder why. Burgundy, yuk.

A new school had just been built also and when I was going into year five, I started in this school. I really didn't mind as it was exciting being in a new house and now a new school, but I did have to make new friends and it was still rather unsettling.

There were only our direct neighbours – The Rainers: Mr and Mrs Rainer, Bobby and Lynette next door; and the O'Briens who lived directly across the road. They lived in a caravan on their patch of land while they built their house. The O'Briens took me to see my first grown up movie, *South Pacific*, in the city. Gosh, I felt so grown up. Their children, Rodney and Louise were a bit older than me, so we were friends but didn't play with each other often.

I made friends with Bobby and Lynnette, however, and would play with them endlessly. One day Bobby hooked up a crystal set and we would try and communicate with it. We even had a go at hooking up two cans with rope that stretched from Bobby's bedroom, over the fence and through to my bedroom window, with the aim of talking to each other. I can't remember if it worked.

On one occasion, Bobby and I went hunting with his slug gun over his shoulder. He led me along the old Mentone Racecourse and we were shooting at rubbish and old cans along the way. We were trailblazers on a wild adventure.

The old course, overgrown with bushes and weeds, had only become a walking track for the adventurous like us. A slight bend formed up ahead and we followed it, pushing our way through the undergrowth. As we turned the corner a man appeared lying down on the ground.

"Oh hell, is he dead?" I asked Bobby.

"I think so," he replied, his voice wavering slightly. "I think we have killed him." I don't think I have ever run so quickly before with Bobby on my heels, yelling at me to keep going. We kept running until we got home. Then, and only then did we stop and take a breath.

"What are we going to do now, Bobby?" I was shaking and awfully close to tears, frightened by what we had done and what would be done to us when we told our parents.

Before too long the police arrived to see us.

"Where was this man?"

"What time did you say you were there?"

"What were you doing there?"'

"I am so sorry," I blurted out. "We didn't mean to do it."

"Do what?"

Bobby had gone red in the face, and I must admit he looked anything but the brave hunter he was on our adventure. He, too, had started shaking and was biting his lip in an effort to hold back the tears. "We were only shooting at old cans and rubbish," he blurted. "We didn't even see him there."

"I think you had better show us where this all happened. Do you think you can remember where it was?" the policeman sternly asked.

We both agreed. We knew where it was but as we went to follow the policemen out to the car, they turned to me and said it might be best if I stayed at home.

This really wasn't fair I thought, *just 'cos I was a girl*, but I did as I was told and went inside wondering what was going to happen to Bobby and me. Would we go to jail? Did they lock up kids like us? Who was the man and had he really been dead?

When Bobby returned home the policemen came in to speak to our parents.

"Was he really dead?" I whispered to Bobby.

"Yep."

As it turned out and was evidenced, the old man had not been shot by us. He had wandered off from the Heatherton Sanitorium and stumbled, falling headfirst into a puddle. Cause of death was drowning! That was an eventful day indeed and our parents suggested we just play with the slug gun in the back yard from then on, as you did in those days!

♦

One day as I was walking home from school with my friend, Cheryl, I turned the corner and I noticed there were a lot of cars parked outside my house. My grandfather was approaching me. I don't know how I already knew, but I did. I froze on the spot.

My grandfather asked Cheryl to go on ahead.

"No! Don't tell me!" I screamed at him. I wanted to run along with Cheryl. I wanted to snap out of this nightmare. For I knew, deep down inside, that my father had died.

I ran past my grandfather, straight into the house, straight into my room. I was screaming as if my own life depended on it. Howling and howling, I could not bear the news. I was aware of others in the house, specifically in the lounge room but no one came to see if I was okay. No one came to comfort me. Nothing was said. All I remember was throwing myself on the bed writhing in so much pain that I had not realised my Uncle Mike's presence beside me. I have no memory of what he said or did, for suddenly I was no longer there. I went to another place.

I have zero recollection for a good period of time after my father died. I must have gone to live with Aunty Nan, Uncle Mick and my cousins. Why? I did not know. For how long? I have no idea. I only recall one evening when Aunty Nan was serving dinner. My cousins were there, and we were sharing fish fingers, mashed potatoes, peas and raw grated carrots sprinkled on top. To this day I still enjoy that same combination.

Obviously, I was aware that I lived with them but I didn't know why or how that had come to be. It didn't really cross my mind, to be honest. The days rolled by; some days with my cousins, other days they went to school. But I was always home, and it never occurred to me as to why I didn't go to school with them. One day I found myself hiding in the hall, listening to Aunty Nan talking to Mum on the phone. Even though I could hear every word, none of it made any sense to me. I was still stationed in my other place.

Eventually I was sent home to live with my mother and two sisters again yet I've no defining moment of this change. It just took place. I was just home again. Or was I?

Nothing seemed real and I understand now why Poppet came to be with me. I couldn't make sense of this new life so she took over for me. She found it hard to cope sometimes but I alone would have had no hope at all. She has since told me that when she asked my mother why I hadn't gone to my father's funeral, my mother replied, "I was too young". She did not even tell Poppet where my father was buried and suggested that perhaps it was a good idea not to talk about him anymore.

A kind-hearted man from down the road upcycled an old bike for me. Some of the neighbours pitched in and they painted it blue with a lovely shine. I was gifted the bike for the Christmas that followed my father's passing and when I got on that bike, I was as free as the wind. Free from all the pain, confusion and loss. I now acknowledge that Poppet was a constant companion throughout these bleakest of times. She carried on for me. She carried the weight.

Bobby, Poppet and I rode our bikes to the Moorabbin airport to watch the small planes take off and land. It was a rather small airport, but it was very busy. We attended air shows and actually got to sit in the planes, imagining soaring off to exotic places.

Then an Egyptian family moved in down the road. Mrs Coridius was always preparing something delicious like almond biscuits covered in icing sugar or orange slices marinated in syrup. Their son, Con, announced to his mother that he loved me and gave me a plastic skull-and-crossbones ring, salvaged from a liquorice strap. But I developed a crush on Campbell, the new kid in town. He looked like Cliff Richard and when he said hello to me, I would blush tomato red.

"How sad to lose her daddy like that," were the sentiments the neighbourhood expressed and I felt their empathy but it had happened to another girl, to Isobella, not me, so even though I sensed their compassion it didn't really affect me. Poppet was carrying all the suffering I had detached and disassociated from. Besides, no one spoke to me about my feelings regarding my father's death. Instead, I was to take care of my mother and help her with my sisters. I was the eldest, after all.

Of course! I was ten. I could do that. That wasn't a problem and so life went on.

I returned to school as though nothing had happened. (Remember, it had all happened to someone else.) I grew fond of school and fell in love with arithmetic and science. I forged a sense of belonging and had a lot of fun really, becoming one of the leaders as a marching girl which is as far as my PE talent got me.

When I came home from school my mother was often there slumped on the coach, subdued from one or three nips of sherry. I knew it was my job to look after her and my sisters, to be the responsible eldest child, so if I could stop my mother from being sad, then that was the least I could do. My sisters retaliated when I told them what to do but I learnt to get on with the job regardless. At night I would cry myself to sleep after carrying all the weight of them repeatedly telling me I was not their mother and why should they do what I say.

Mum did pull herself together at some point. After she found me standing on a stool frying up chips for my sisters' dinner, Nana Mabs was called to get on the next plane out of England to come and help us. Poppet was in a state of confusion juggling all the responsibility but she, too, carried on and together we were comforted by Nana Mabs' presence. She had remembered me after all this time and our bond was still strong.

18 months after my father died, my mother met another man, David Fanning. Poppet and I didn't think too much of it, he was of no consequence to us then. My mother also returned to work as an Insurance Assessor and life was moving in new directions for all of us. David moved in with the family which meant Nana Mabs now had to sleep in my room. Together we would stay up late talking while I painted my nails. How she put up with my Elvis posters, I do not know, for that was when Mizzy, the teenager, had arrived. I do remember many nights when poor Nana was obviously so tired and she would plead with me, "My giddy aunt, Deneeze, let's go to sleep."

There was a sense thing were starting to settle down around the home; normality was piercing through the cracks. I didn't really like David coming to live with us and I let this be known to Mizzy. One evening, my mother threw a dinner party for David's family and friends. It was an introduction of sorts or perhaps for an announcement. Needless to say, it was all a bit overwhelming.

Strangers in my home saying hello to me – no one I could identify with – and I woke the next morning in my pyjamas, in my bed. One minute, surrounded by strangers. The next, back in my bed. When I asked my mother what happened that night, she said, "We found you sitting in the shower giggling your head off, so David put you to bed."

'Shit, shit!' said Mizzy.

"Did he change me into my pyjamas?" I asked.

"Of course he did. I was busy entertaining guests so he said he would do it. Why do you always have to make a fuss about everything?" Her annoyance was clear and put an end to our conversation.

'Shit, shit!' said Mizzy.

I was eleven and a half at the time, developing early and had already had my first period. Not only were my breasts developing but I had pubic hair as well. I was self-conscious of my maturation and mortified that David had changed me. It would have made a huge difference if my mother had stepped in. But she didn't.

And that's when The Nothingess made itself known.

I know Poppet and possibly Mizzy were struggling with all this 'growing-up' business. Sassy One quickly arrived. She didn't like what she saw but thankfully brought with her new coping skills. We were all growing up very quickly and life was becoming more complex. I was somewhere lost in the middle, changing on the outside, multiplying within.

♦

At 11 years of age, I was diagnosed with Depression, not that I was allowed to tell anyone. It wouldn't reflect well on my mother, would it?

'Bad Mummy,' said Poppet.

Shame kicked in alongside it and I started feeling worthless. I didn't mean to be depressed, it just happened. But it was official. I had been taken to the doctors and (with their help) ticked all the boxes:

- ☑ Tiredness
- ☑ Weepy
- ☑ Lethargy
- ☑ Unable to concentrate.
- ☑ A sense of doom and gloom, always
- ☑ Lack of motivation
- ☑ Persistent feeling of sadness

Just take this pill and you'll be all right.

On occasions, when the list grew longer, I would be sent to see a psychiatrist for a second opinion. But it always came back the same – Denise is suffering from Depression. I would take my prescriptive anti-depressant medicine and told to 'see how I went'. If there were any problems, to go back. This set the tone for an on-again-off-again lifetime dance with medication.

The major contender back then was Premenstrual Depression, then later, Postoperative Depression and Postnatal Depression. Other times I was told that I was, put simply, *depressed*, and there was no use of an adjective to justify it. As Annabel once observed, regarding my sense of losing large chunks of time, that the dynamic with my alters was similar to a match of tag-team. This best describes my inner-world during my early teenage years. I always seemed to be causing trouble for my mother and at the same time entering wide stretches of emptiness within.

Whenever I got into trouble with my mother, I'd sink into dark moods of *nothingness* and Quassie would shield me from her angry outbursts. I felt guilty and there was a lot of subtle switching taking place between myself and my alters as though this pattern of behaviour was becoming integrated as a default way of existence. It was difficult to keep track of all the movement.

When I was 12, life changed again and darkness fell upon me with severity. Yet it was a safe place and unbeknownst to me, the others would take over.

We were moving. Why? Because he said so. I didn't like him before. Now it was turning to hate. Poppet was hit hard having her once turned upside-down world turned upside-down again. She wanted to yell and scream. '*No! Don't do this!*

I am beginning to feel again. Please don't make me go!' she cried. But no one heard her and we both receded further into the darkness. I was so lonely and the pain and loss of losing friendships was too much to bear.

Pain and fear settled in a knotted ball in my stomach. I didn't feel safe and secure in the world, I never had been. Instead, I lived in a climate of confusion. I wonder if that chaos is what formed the relentless torment in my stomach that had emerged from the chaos, from being spun out of control. I didn't think I could ever make sense of it.

Not only would I be leaving friends behind but my Nana too. She wasn't part of the new move. David was the one behind this. He said he wanted to make a 'fresh start'. Why couldn't he just take my mother out occasionally? Instead, he was ruining my young life. Would I ever feel as though I *belonged* anywhere?

Eventually, my mother married David. Everyone raved about his good qualities, highlighting all he had done for us as a family. Perhaps I could have been more grateful but it made no difference to me as I simply could not bring myself to like this man. I held him responsible for destroying my life even though he provided security for my mother.

When the day arrived for them to be married, I appeared to have upset my mother again – I hated the dress she was making me wear and I told her so. Everyone else seemed to be happy.

"I hate this dress, Mum. Do I really have to wear it?" I think Poppet was using the dress as an excuse for why I was so miserable.

"Why do you always have to be so difficult, Denise? I am not listening to you today. I am getting married and even you can't spoil it for me."

And so, I dissociated.

Quassie allowed for my disappearance, and I recall zilch about the wedding. Into the depths of *nothingness* I dissolved. He seemed to do this on a regular basis back then, for I never intended on being disruptive and yet I was always getting into trouble. I didn't think life could get worse after that.

But it did.

♦

The time that we moved marked the time David began touching and kissing me whenever he could pin me down alone. I recall him coming towards me down the hallway, a look in his eyes I cannot shake. He would reach out for me then kiss me with his pudgy, wet and unwelcome lips. The revulsion has stayed with me but the details of these events, I forget.

When I struggled to flee, he would grasp me tighter, pressing his body against mine. I'd felt nothing of the sort before and I instinctively knew it was wrong. I had no idea what an erection was then but I knew when he was pressing against me it was not normal and that compounded all the confusion.

His heavy breathing, his touch upon my breasts, his voice whispering to me how beautiful they were – I wanted to vomit while screaming on the inside. How could he do this to me? My attempts to break free were always futile and the seething mix of feelings it triggered, unnameable.

What about my mother? How could he do this if he loved her? I knew telling her would break her heart and so I internalised the experience further. How I loathed this man, his hands, his intention. My *nothingness* became my saving grace.

It was soon decided that David would adopt us.

This involved my mother giving up her children to become wards of the state for 12 months. We still lived at home and while the adoption was being processed our legal guardian was Reverend Muxworthy. Before the adoption by David was finalised, we all had to be present in court.

Myra, Kerrie and I were taken by ourselves to be with the judge in his chambers. He enquired, "Is it okay for David to adopt you?"

Kerrie was sitting on the judge's knee and Myra stood beside him. Could either of them comprehend what he was asking? Kerrie was four and a half years old. She just smiled.

I wanted to scream, *No! It's not okay!*

Silenced was my voice. Poppet remained quiet. I felt helpless and so did she.

I was no longer Denise Perkins, I was Denise Fanning.

We were taken to a Chinese restaurant in the city to celebrate.

♦

If I were rude to David, my mother would tell me I was naughty. The sexual abuse continued, and I was continually getting into trouble. But I wouldn't dare dream of telling her how mixed-up, afraid and upset I was for she was happy and was no longer crying. I was doing my job by looking after her. End of story.

The narrative with David continued to unfold in twisted ways. I asked him many times over the years why he kept doing this to me and pleaded for him to stop.

"If only you could love me as your sisters do," he would whisper in my ear. "Then I wouldn't have to."

It was my fault. My fault. My fault.

Whenever his wet lips smothered me, I felt excruciatingly sick in my stomach. The only escape was my black hole – my tunnel of *nothingness* – and my alters who stepped in to protect me. I'm unsure as to how they managed, but heroically they saved me from the sordid details of his ruthless abuse.

Once, when I was washing my hair in the shower, I stood rinsing out the shampoo and as I opened my eyes he was there, leaning against the door, arms crossed, just staring at me. *Leering* would be the more accurate term. This repulsive face, staring at my naked body. When I reached for the washcloth to cover myself and hide my breasts with my other arm, he said, "Don't do that." Almost pleading. "I just want to look at you. You are so beautiful."

I was sickened by his presence, feeling all but beautiful at the time and edging closer to vomit.

'I hate him! I hate him!' I surrendered my rage to the *nothingness.* I was engulfed by the blackness. It was welcome for now. He could not touch me there.

It was *my nothingness.*

He left, quietly closing the door behind him and I burst into tears not caring who heard. No one ever did. No one ever came. No one would even know that something was wrong with me.

♦

There were times, however, that I pondered whether I was the one who had it all wrong and was I just being silly? On Sunday evenings we would have fresh sandwiches and a cream cake in the lounge room, all the while enjoying watching the tellie. David would take a shower and rather than taking a change of clothes with him, would run past the sliding doors on his way to the bedroom, accidently, on purpose, dropping the towel behind him. He would stand there, naked, for us all to see.

Mum, Myra and Kerrie would laugh, saying how funny it all was every bloody time he did it. I was sickened and found the whole shebang repulsive. Myra was still only five and Kerrie, no older than three. It wasn't funny, it was disgusting.

At the age of 14 I became sexually involved with a man called Don Oke. He was David's partner in business, 35 years old. Married, with two sons. This lasted a year and it was during my involvement with Don that Sassy One joined the group. She was happy that someone seemed to really love us; love us all at last.

I told my girlfriend at the time that I felt as though I was leading a 'double life' as Don would sometimes pick me up from the bus stop and drive me to school. Awful things occurred during those rides in his car. I know they did but I cannot remember. For as soon as I felt his hands touching me below my skirt, I would panic and flee to the *nothingness*. It could have been either Poppet or Sassy One who dealt with Don.

Other days I'd catch the school bus like all the other students. I would be the 'normal' teenager checking out the boys from Mentone Boys Grammar school, giggling with my girlfriends. My 'double life' continued throughout my teens and I grew increasingly ashamed, dirty, guilty, confused, lonely, with nowhere to turn. Except, of course, to my *nothingness* despite how bleak and empty it was there.

I can't thank my alters enough for all that they dealt with back then, unbeknownst to me. My life had become a permanent nightmare that never seemed to end. The twisted knot in my stomach could not be resolved and there are countless blanked out moments I cannot recall. The relationship with my mother continued to erode. I can now understand why Quassie emerged so battered and bruised from my youth. He certainly took many a verbal beating from her and her undealt rage. With a heavy sense of gloom, I tried to participate in family activities, switching subtly but frequently between my alters. Poppet and Isobella longed for the simplicity of the early years and Mizzy gave me the strength to say *no*, when needed.

Yet I had no idea this was happening at the time. Although at times it was defining and I could observe myself disappear into the *nothingness*, the tone of the years was one of chaos and confusion.

Mizzy once said, *'Your mind could be likened to a washing machine, rinsing and spinning around and around.'*

And she was right.

I would struggle to get out of bed, to which my mother would say, "You just need a stick of ginger up your bum... for goodness sake, stop feeling sorry for yourself!"

I later learned that the ginger technique helped racehorses run faster, which was such a departure from where I stood. I could barely manage a slow walk. My sense of worthlessness dragged me into an oblivion. I somehow managed to do well at school and yearned to be a 'normal' teenager but the truth was, I was a mess. My life felt completely out of my control in a mire of powerlessness and debilitating confusion. God help us all! How the hell did my guys feel if I felt this way?

Each day I'd promise myself to get organised, pay attention, be a good girl, as per Logical One's advice but my reports always said the same thing: *She would do much better if she concentrated and paid more attention.* I was anything but organised and it showed. Always daydreaming, forgetting homework, getting lost in all the noise within my head. These sacred promises I continually made to myself proved futile. Tomorrow was never going to be another day. The constant tugging and pulling of my alters competing for attention, it tired me to the bone. I was trapped between different times, places, memories, voices.

That's right, I was *depressed*!

This was the Depression talking.

I've heard people say their high school years were some of the best days of their life.

This could not be further from my truth.

♦

A lot happened in my sixteenth year.

I started joining social groups and outwardly appeared to be having fun going to parties with boys, getting up to harmless, teenage mischief here and there but David always lurked in the background. It was also the year I had my first suicide attempt, got my first job, met my first husband and, unbeknownst at the time, welcomed another alter into existence.

My physical health was under scrutiny. The stomach pains were worsening to the point where I needed medical examination. The doctor diagnosed me with appendicitis and within two hours I was to have my appendix removed. It was the middle of winter and both my mother and David escorted me to the hospital. I resented that David was there and would have much preferred to just be with my mother. I was in hospital for two weeks and told the operation had been quite tricky. I spent three weeks at home in convalescence before returning to school, at which point I was overwhelmed having fallen behind in all my studies.

I found myself fretting over whether the doctor had revealed to my mother that I was no longer a virgin. Mizzy's analogy of the washing machine, of the relentless ruminations rinsing and spinning around my head caused me immense headaches. I didn't want to think anymore as that seemed to compound the imploding sensations. One evening, in an effort to cope, I took to screaming into my pillow. "Just make it all stop!" I yelled repeatedly. The voices, the noises, the panic, the thoughts; I believed I was losing my mind.

My mother came to investigate and when she arrived at the foot of my bed she said, "What the hell is the matter with you?" She seemed more annoyed than concerned about my sudden outburst.

I was sobbing in distress. I had no idea what was wrong with me and blurted out that I had been seeing Don Oke for twelve months. I felt sick and ashamed, purging the story from within. What ensued left me feeling shattered.

My mother expressed grave disappointment and said, "For goodness sake, don't tell your father. It will break his heart." She turned away and left me alone. I was stunned with remorse and so much anger.

It was during this time that Janice came to the fore. I later discovered that it was decided by my team of alters that I was too weak to carry the weight of anger brewing in the pit of my stomach, so Janice stepped in to help out. I lived in fear of what might happen if I were to express my rage, so she absorbed the load, in essence, sweeping it all under the carpet for me as the anger continued to fester. I stewed over why Mum never told the police about Don. Never game to ask her why, I would have been straight to the police if a teenager had reported anything of the sort. It was rape. I was only 14 when Don stated, and he was supposedly a responsible adult who should not have done this. This brought up further questioning.

Did she know David was abusing me? And if so, did she fear the consequences if the truth was exposed? What would the neighbours say? And the women at the Golf Club? Being married to a paedophile was not a good look in the slightest, was it? The situation drove me deeper into my *nothingness;* there was no escaping the nightmare that was my life, the stacked-up pain, abuse, suffering, neglect, unworthiness, turmoil, and inner-chaos. So I turned to suicide. A woeful first attempt at shutting it all down. Six antihistamines later, all I had was a rejuvenating sleep. Indeed, there was no solution within reach to combat the battle that was my pure existence.

♦

Year 11 exams came and went, and I failed all of them despite my diligent efforts to catch up after my operation. Mum would often find me asleep at my desk late at night and would usher me into bed. The shock of discovering I had failed was too much to bear and added to the already firmly established unworthiness inside me; another trigger and opportunity to revert to the *nothingness* yet again.

There was never any conversation with my mother about returning to school having failed but instead she enrolled me in the new year in a receptionist course at Suzanne Johnsons. I had been dreaming of attending university and furthering my studies and interest in science, yet this was overruled by my mother's decision that I was better suited to a receptionist job and clearly those aspirations were unobtainable. It was easier to just go along with her by this stage, since my faculties of thought and free will had rapidly declined.

Much to my surprise Suzanne Johnsons encouraged me to enter the Victorian Miss Teenage Quest, an opportunity that reignited a mere spark of excitement and sense of pride.

"Don't get too carried away, it's just a fundraising scheme," my mother said, which of course I knew but she had burst my hopeful bubble and I felt stupid for even caring.

I went on to participate in some of the fundraising events, one of them being a fashion show. It gave me the opportunity to buy a new outfit and parade along a catwalk. I felt so grown up in my matching apricot dress and jacket. People applauded me and I felt valued, for a moment.

"You did well," my mother said, "but why on Earth did you pick that colour? It did nothing for you."

I had grown so used to my mother's diminishing comments that to hear words of encouragement or genuine care were but a pipe dream. I was already entrenched in feeling isolated in the world without any real sense of who I was, that being lost, lonely and bloody confused all the time was really all I knew how to be.

♦

We were encouraged from the very first day of the course to apply for as many jobs as we could, to gain experience. After the end of the 1st day, I noticed an advertisement in a shop front window. Suzanne Johnson was located at the top end of Collins Street which was at the time dotted with elite and exclusive boutiques, finance corporations and medical specialists. It was Mizzy who saw the opportunity for what it could be, who went ahead and applied for the job!

'Good! One job application done,' she thought as we headed for the train station to catch our ride home.

When I arrived home, I was greeted by mother saying, "Someone has just phoned for you and said you have been accepted for the job." I had no idea what she was talking about. Who had phoned? What was the job? I was befuddled and disbelieving.

"They want you to call them as soon as possible." She handed me a piece of paper with their number written on it, so obligingly I made the call.

"Hello, my name is Denise Fanning. I was to ring you when I got home?"

"Great, Denise," a voice down the phone said. "We have considered you for the receptionist role and we would like to offer you the position. We were wondering, when can you start?"

I explained I was finishing up a course for the next two

weeks and they were pleased for me to commence then.

I hung up the phone, relieved to have bought myself some time to wrap my head around this new arrangement. I had no recollection of what they were talking about. The next day as I walked up Collins Street on my way to Suzanne Johnsons, I spotted the notice on the shopfront window of OPSM and pieced together the events that had followed. Mizzy had applied for the job on behalf of me, it seemed. Vaguely I made sense of the process. Suzanne Johnsons seemed quite surprised when I announced my new role as Receptionist for OPSM Head Office. I'll never forget my first pay packet of $16.96. Somehow, I was moving up in the world. I paid a third to my mother for board, purchased my train ticket and paid health insurance. With the meagre amount remaining I lay-buyed a coat. The first grown-up coat I'd ever owned.

Thank you, Mizzy.

♦

Meeting Ian, my first experience of a primary relationship with a man, brought with it its own set of interesting circumstances. Our paths had crossed at a social event back when I was sixteen. He clearly fancied me, all the while winking at me from across the restaurant, even though I was with a boyfriend at the time. I was bemused but also a little flattered.

A little further down the track I received a call from him, inviting me out to the movies. I no longer had a boyfriend so agreed to see *The Bible* – a long and boring film punctuated with tentative moves towards holding hands. Mizzy and I were thrilled to be having this experience, although I still remained in a liminal space of nothing seeming quite real. Ian introduced me to his friends, Ray and Carmel (who to this day I am still friends with), and we continued dating for what seemed a good year or so.

During my time with OPSM, I grew tired of commuting to the city as it was extremely uncomfortable travelling on the old red rattler trains during the cold mornings or hot summer days. They were usually overcrowded and smelt putrid with stale air, body odour and smoking in the mix. My state of enduring lethargy continued while I plodded along, disconnected and disengaged from the world happening around me.

Ian, Ray, Carmel and I formed a tight group, often travelling to the country together and taking road trips. It was around the time of the Vietnam War that Ian and Ray had first met and they worked for the Citizen Military Force (CMF). I was impressed with their uniform and felt glowingly proud when we were out with them, bar one occasion on ANZAC Day. I'll never forget that day!

Carmel and I were only seventeen at the time and thought it would be a hoot to run alongside the ANZAC parade yelling out their names. They didn't even look our way, so we called even louder. We were blind to the solemnity of the occasion and when it ended and we reunited with our men, they reproached us sternly for sorely embarrassing them. This was not the only time I had embarrassed Ian, which developed into a pattern of sorts throughout our relationship.

Like the time we were dining out and I ordered escargot. I saved the biggest one until last. Many have spoken of the horror of this incident occurring for indeed, my snail went flying across the room as the 'slippery little sucker' shot from the tight grip of my clasp. It was supposed to be a romantic dinner. Ian turned red in the face. But it was what happened next that mortified him and was beyond my conscious control.

I stood up from the table and proceeded asking others in the room if they had seen my snail.

'They can move so fast when they make up their minds, can't they?!' exclaimed Mizzy. I would never have been so bold as to say such a thing. Everyone was amused, except Ian, who abruptly ended dinner and took me home.

On the day of my eighteenth birthday, I passed my driving licence test. This was a significant turning point for I had been considering joining the Navy as a driver and leaving behind my work as a receptionist for good. Ian, Ray and Carmel all joined me in a visit to the Naval Base in Hastings just to take a look around. It was so exciting for me so I went ahead and booked an interview and a medical assessment, however I quickly learned that I could not join as a driver until I was nineteen or had held my license for at least 12 months.

Since both outcomes occurred on the same date, the decision I needed to make was between waiting until then to enlist, which meant I would need to continue working as a receptionist or join the Navy now and transfer when I was eligible to become a driver. When I discussed my options with Ian he flatly told me that if I were to join the Navy then I shouldn't expect him to hang around.

So why had he bothered coming to Hastings with me and why didn't he bring this up before the inductions? Had he not been taking me seriously all that time? I was perplexed and questioned if he was being that serious, yet he was adamant. If I were to join the Navy, he would split. If not, he said he would marry me. I was caught in an ultimatum that required of me a lot of thinking *and* discussion with my team; the thought of both things overwhelmed and tired me further. So under the carpet I swept the situation with the hope it might magically sort itself out, when my dilemma was thwarted by a new advertised position for a Courier Driver.

The salary was too good to be true and it would mean I could quickly start driving as I wished. I rang the agency straight away to arrange an interview and next minute, they hired me! I was then to become the second female Courier Driver in Melbourne for the elite company, Downards. I was fitted for a uniform – a red mini skirt with a matching vest and cream coloured shirt. Talk about style and class!

Driving for Downards seemed too good to be true and my desire to join the Navy was quickly forgotten. I had many adventures in my mini-minor van sporting psychedelic, colourful patterns on it with red lettering loudly displaying *Downards.* Ian was happy that I had not joined the Navy and I was happy enough to still be with him. I learned not to take myself seriously as the slightly embarrassing moments that occurred in the company of Ian were spilling over into my new job as a courier.

On my first day I heard them call 201 on the two-way radio. This was my call number and it sounded muffled through the radio, I responded and was given my next address.

"201" it sounded through the muffled speaker. I responded and was given my next address.

"Thank you, Pat," I said.

The voice sounded back down the two-way, "That's a Roger 201."

"Oh, sorry! Thank you, Roger," I replied.

The following day my colleague explained that 'Roger' was the sign-off code for the radio. My error amused a lot of male drivers I'm sure but none more so than the two men who worked in the main dispatch office who greeted me with hurling laughter. They were doubled over with jocularity. I giggled along, taking it all on the chin.

Another perplexing instance of confounder occurred when I was delivering a carton of very expensive champagne to a VIP client in an affluent suburb of Melbourne. I was not allowed to carry any heavy deliveries, as was this one, so made my way empty-handed to the front door. When I rang the bell, I could see a man heading towards me through the frosted glass panels. He opened the door, appearing half shaven on the face with a smother of lotion down one cheek and only wearing a robe.

I quickly apologised and said I would call in another time, to which he responded, "Don't be silly, just give me a minute, I'll be right out."

He re-appeared with his face whipped clean but still sporting his robe. He followed me to the van to help with the carton. As he leant forward to lift it, his robe came undone at the strap and I was privy to his stark-naked body, there and then! He smiled but I was shocked and began hiccupping, relentlessly.

"Oh dear," he said. "Would you like to come in for a glass of water?"

"No thank you," I declined. "I just ate a sandwich and I get hiccups after eating fresh bread. I'm fine." Unsure of whether he believed me, I tried to vanish into my van and quickly backed out of his driveway. I wasn't game enough to look back.

It was during my employment with Downards that Ian moved into a new flat on his own, however on one particular day I arrived at my own home to be greeted by my mother, who explained that Ian was there and upstairs in bed.

"Why?" I queried. "Why wasn't he in his own bed at the flat and why was he not at work?"

Mum explained he was very unwell and had arrived there in agony saying he was in incredible pain, grumbling about an appendix.

When the doctor came to assess him, he advised my mother that Ian was having a stomach migraine and prescribed medication to settle it. Mum had already collected it from the chemist and given it to Ian, who was now asleep. I asked no further questions and let Ian just be, when low and behold, he ended up living with my mother for another eight weeks.

It was an odd time. I would go to work leaving Ian in bed and Mum would look after him for the day. Often, I would come home to find them chatting in the kitchen or lounging about drinking coffee on the couch. Their bond was clearly strengthening and it was not uncommon that they would go out shopping together or for lunch. Mum even taught him how to play golf, after which they would come home bantering about their game.

I can best describe my position amongst the familiarity

and closeness shared by them as being demoted to the third wheel. Mum even commented that Ian was like the son she never had, yet when we eventually announced our engagement, she was very much against it.

Again, I was left feeling perplexed, unsure. Bewildered.

♦

How and why I became engaged to Ian was cause for further confusion. It just seemed to happen, like everything did in my life. I only remember anecdotal snippets of fleeting events. The proposal was much the same. We were taking some of his extra clothes to the new flat.

We bought Chinese take-away afterwards for dinner and ate it in the carpark at Rickets Point. The bayside view remains a clear picture in my mind.

I'm not sure how it began or what it was about but we had a horrendous argument and my head was pounding with excruciating pain. It was much later on that I learned these headaches were actual physiological disturbances caused by the switching of my alters; subtle changes affecting the neurological activity in my brain. I had reached breaking point by the bay that night and started walking along the water's edge, when I heard myself repeating an old saying:

I stood on a hill at midnight,
When a thought came into my head.
What the hell was I doing there,
When I could have been in bed?

Precisely, what the hell was I doing there? It was dark,

the bay was deserted, and I was a long way from home, so I turned back and headed to the car insistent that Ian be the one to drive us. When I got back to the car there he was, leaning back on the bonnet telling me how lucky I had been that I had come back when I did. He had a knife and was holding it to his chest. It was a plastic knife from the takeaway shop but a knife, nonetheless.

"I was so close to killing myself!" he announced.

God no, I thought to myself. *I couldn't have carried any more guilt.*

I quickly forgave him and found myself instantly agreeing to marry him.

Everything's a blur thereafter as so many of the voices were chiming in with their conflicting views but this was how the engagement eventuated, all cluttered, disjointed, under pressure. As fleeting and effervescent as a dream; as fast did the moment arrive did it vanish from my recollection, as did the stories within stories of my muddled life.

♦

We married on the 17th of April 1971. I was nineteen, a week off turning twenty and it was as though it was all happening to somebody else. You could describe it as an out-of-body experience, a common symptom of DID.

We had ventured to Bright for our honeymoon, a beautiful part of regional Victoria and the autumn leaves falling created a picturesque time of year. The landscape was magnificent, however on the first day of our honeymoon so many thoughts were running through my mind. I recognise now, in hindsight, that all my alters were arguing relentlessly amongst themselves and I had stunned myself with my actions. What the hell had I done?

I was no longer Denise Fanning. I had become Denise Young and on the first day of this new existence I cried uncontrollably, the tears only ceasing when I fell asleep.

After the honeymoon I lived with Ian in his flat and it was as though I was playing a role in a theatrical production. My character was emotionless. My surrounds, surreal. No one seemed aware of this distorted reality I was trapped in, and I was expert at hiding any hint of abnormality. Me and my 'stiff upper lip' plodded along through married life even though I wasn't really all there. I had become *The Great Pretender.*

We bought our first home together around the corner from Mum and David and decided to have a baby. But that was not so straightforward. We had been trying for two and a half years until my mother divulged to me that my appendix operation had in truth, been the removal of one of my ovaries.

"What?! Why the hell hadn't I been told this?" I yelled at her.

"We didn't want you to worry about it," was all she said.

I was in disbelief of her excuse and angry that my right to know that this had happened to my body, had been betrayed... by my own mother. I decided to educate myself further on what this might mean, finding some research that indicated it could have been a benign tumour. It was actually a dermoid cyst.

Once the initial shock had passed, I thought how cruel it was of my mother to withhold such important information from me for so long, as she knew I was desperately trying to conceive. She could have told me sooner; saved me the years of trying, hoping, praying to fall pregnant. Now that I knew, I went to see a doctor who said pregnancy was not a certainty, either way, and that I should consider adoption, sending me home with lots of paperwork to consider.

I didn't want to think about it. I was still infuriated with my mother. Again, another significant issue in my life swept under the carpet, out of sight. It was Janice who held all this unprocessed rage for me as I could not have coped with confrontation with my mother. Janice absorbed it all.

Sometime later though, it did occur to me that perhaps Ian and I should consider adoption if we were serious about having a child under these circumstances. He must have agreed – I don't entirely remember – but I do remember tackling the many forms! It was a laborious effort with my headaches on the return. When out of the blue, as if by miracle, we conceived.

I'll never forget the first appointment with my gynaecologist. He was feeling my tummy. Stepping back, with a smile on his face, he looked me directly in the eye and said, "Denise, you know and I know you are pregnant, so could you please just relax and stop pushing out your tummy."

Gee, I felt stupid but overjoyed with excitement. Nonetheless. I was going to be having a baby!

♦

The news spread quickly with nary a word mentioned about the secret my mother had kept from me all those years. I loved being pregnant and carried well, never suffering morning sickness. The only time it caused me any grief was one time in the swimming pool. I had rolled onto my back and could not get upright. Someone had to jump in to turn me over and drag me poolside.

'Yeah, bit like a beached whale!' Mizzy joked. I suppose I am glad she always showed me the funny side.

I could no longer drive for Downards and returned to my receptionist skills, fulfilling their front desk duties at Head Office. I found the old plug-and-chord switchboards terribly confusing. I would panic, plugging chords here and there in all the wrong outlets, huffing and puffing then gaining composure. No one ever said anything. I suppose I was the token pregnant woman, fumbling as I grew rotund.

Six months into my pregnancy I decided to get a dog and visited a shelter to pick one up. It was a revolting environment, dirty and unkempt with dogs jumping everywhere, barking and wagging and wanting to be loved. As I turned to flee the god-awful place, I noticed a small black creature sitting against a wall. I knew there and then I could not leave it behind. I think I paid $10 and it was Isobella who held this little black bundle home, all snuggled up and fast asleep in my arms.

But something wasn't right, so upon a visit to the vet we discovered she had distemper. "I don't think she will survive the night," the vet informed us.

'No! He has to help her!' Isobella cried. Poppet moved by her side to comfort her.

"Leave her with us and we'll keep her under observation tonight," said the vet, who could see I was in such a state of distress.

I called the next day to discover she had survived and

went to bring her home with a batch of medicines. Well Tinker, who was possibly like a first child, she just thrived with all my nurturance. My maternal instincts had kicked in and she became a much-loved member of our family. (She lived to the ripe old age of sixteen and a half.)

♦

My daughter, Jodie, was born in February 1974. A beautiful baby girl. Life was at its best. On the surface, of course. My sense of not belonging continued as the undercurrent of my existence. Motherhood was going on around me but I was never really present. Each day rolled into the next. Jodie grew and flourished, then (however some years later) I discovered I was pregnant with our second child. Never thinking I would be lucky enough to have another, the news made me very happy, and Ian and I started building a new house in Dingley to accommodate our growing family. Corey was born in the winter of 1976. The hospital stay was seamless but when I returned home, everything fell apart.

Something was very wrong with me. More wrong than I had ever noticed.

We were living in a rental property, and I felt no connection with the real world at all. I couldn't focus. Half the time, I had no idea where I was. It was as though I had fallen down a steep, black hole and the world was staged above me. I was not a part of it. I was completely out of touch with reality and if I attempted to yell for help, I found I had no voice.

'Where is that baby?' Marm would ask.

'Which baby?' Poppet probed.

'The one that was crying!'

They were a strange blessing in disguise during this time, my team of alters. I would go looking for my baby and there he appeared, atop of the packing boxes in the spare room, bundled up in his carry cot. I would recognize him instantly and hold him tight against my chest. The shroud of guilt that folded in on me for having forgotten about him was a greater weight than that which fell before.

♦

During this dark patch of time, I found that if anyone dared ring me I would scurry to the couch and curl up in a ball, rocking myself while crying, willing the phone to stop ringing. I was quickly diagnosed with Post Natal Depression and prescribed more medication into my mix, but this time warned that it could take up to six weeks for any of it to kick in and I would be able to function again normally. I rolled along as I had learned to do many times before, with no sense of control or will, just going with the motions.

The newly-built house was ready for us to move in, but I have zero memory of the move or how we settled. Corey would have been five months old, and Jodie was three. Tinker continued to lighten up our home as a dog does. I thought it might be a good idea for me to try breeding dogs myself so we bought a beagle bitch called Bebee, as that was all young Corey could pronounce. "Bebee need sleep," I would say and he would follow my instructions to leave her alone.

Tinker and Bebee formed a naturally strong bond as did the children and there was a lot of love circling between them. We mated Bebee with a dog from the kennels which in turn, blessed our home with three delightful puppies. It broke my heart to sell them – I found the whole process unbearable – so my breeding career ended there. I found it awfully taxing consoling Isobella over the matter as she had formed such a strong bond with animals since day dot. I had so much on my plate, caring for kids, and dogs and her. I had Bebee spayed and made the most of her being a beloved part of the household.

These days carried a sweet and secure semblance of normality covering the underlying tension and disconnection that existed deep within myself. My soul was still buried elsewhere, residing in the vast empty fields of *nothingness.*

♦

By the time I'd reached early adulthood, the many blows I'd taken since the loss of my father – the abuse, neglect, abrupt changes and alienation – had all eaten away at my self-worth and sense of belonging in the world, and the carpet under which everything got swept, God only knows how it always had room for more. The exhausting stress of raising babies while trudging beneath a thick cloak of depression; my ongoing departure from reality as I leaned deeper into the *nothingness,* emerging only to tread water through the day-to-day demands. My team of voices circling inside me with their conflicting views, firm opinions, their own baggage. The loss of time flailing in and out of the present moment... I seemed to drift through realms and realities with no will or wherewithal to do much about my mental health. I just kept rolling with the punches, growing a thick husk over my entire being. It formed resilience and a buffer to enduring even more.

I had harboured a lot of resentment for Ian over the

years who was now closer to my parents than I ever was, that when it came time to part ways after 11 years, I was numb to the repercussions. I was a smoker back then and decided to see a hypnotherapist to help me give up. It wasn't working and the hypnotherapist asked if I had any other problems. Well, where do I start? I just told him I was unhappy within my marriage.

We had marriage counselling after that and he said during a group session, "I really don't know why you are so unhappy, Denise. I have spoken with Ian as you know, and it seems that you have a perfect marriage. He doesn't abuse you. He provides for you and is a good father to Jodie and Corey."

But then went on to say, "As I have said, Denise, you seem to have little to complain about but I cannot stress this enough, if you don't leave him, you are going to be physically ill." So that was that! I continued smoking but gave up marriage instead. This marriage had lasted eleven years.

When we told my mother the news, her response was, "How could you do this, Denise? What about Ian and the children? It's always been about you, hasn't it?"

I suppose I had hidden how unhappy I was so well (or was perpetually ignored) that no one seemed to understand my position. Ian just sat on the couch looking very smug and very much sided with my folks. Trying to contain Janice during these moments was near impossible. I felt like the ex-daughter in-law from this point onwards.

When people asked me why I ended the relationship with Ian, I would say, "I already had two children. I didn't need a third." I had simply had enough and while it was not the smoothest of separations it set me free in a small way. Deep down I was never convinced it would work with him and I knew I did not love him anymore. I was reminded of a Buddhist quote that quite simply summed up my sentiments:

When the love has gone, the karmic debt has been paid.

♦

A series of unfortunate events lead me to meeting my second husband. I had a close call in a horrific, fatal car accident and on the same day, arrived home to discover I had been robbed. It was Detective Colin G, a friendly chap who took on my case, who just so happened to be next in line for my second marriage – not that I, as usual, had much of a say in it.

By this time, Sassy One was at the forefront of my alters and sought comfort in intimate relationships. Detective Colin was over-extending his duties, calling me during his night shift to check in on me, keeping me thoroughly updated on my case. One night he asked if Jodie and Corey would like to visit the police station and take a look around. I agreed to the excursion and a number of coffee dates, although did not read the cues. I was a little over seven years older than him and as it was, he was married. When he leant to kiss me over coffee one evening, I was startled but I liked it.

It was while I was vacuuming the house one day and the phone rang, that Colin announced, "Get the kettle on. I have just left Christine and I am on my way over."

'Oh, bloody hell! Here we go again!' said Sassy One, quietly slinking into the background.

'What on earth did he mean, he just left Christine?' enquired Mizzy. *'Why did I not know that?'*

And why didn't I just say no? I couldn't. I simply couldn't. I didn't want to hurt his feelings and again, seemed lost in a frenzy of voices. This man had just left his wife for me. I was feeling sickly and couldn't think straight. Biting my lip in a whirlwind of confusion, I paced from one room to the next. Hell's bells! I didn't think I loved him that much. *Here we go again anyway.* I allowed for him to move in straight away, all on a whim, which is how my life played out. Out of control. Disconnected from reality. I escaped into my void space and allowed my team to run the show. Dissociating led me aimlessly down winding roads again.

I attracted more abuse. Colin turned out to be an emotionally abusive and a very controlling person, and no matter what happened, everything was my fault when life didn't go his way. It was like living with a dry alcoholic; I never knew which Col would come through the door, and he caused trouble between myself, my children, and my family. There were many occasions I was dragged home from social engagements, berated for supposedly humiliating him; instances where I had lost control but I had no idea what I was doing. I lived in a whirlwind of Mizzy and Poppet and mayhem without anyone knowing what that was like, for I didn't really understand either. I was not yet aware of my *Unknown Friends Within.* Had I grasped them as a concept I may have handled things differently.

My mother didn't like Colin but I followed him around like a puppy, reluctantly deciding to buy property together. Me and my team were drowning in the big decisions. I was sure of nothing. The narrative in my head made me giddy. It was easier to just go along with it.

"This is the one," Colin said, and I surrendered, handing

over all my savings.

'You are pathetic,' said Mizzy.

'What the hell did you do that for?' Logical One asked.

'I don't know what to say anymore. I don't like fighting anymore,' said Poppet.

Then when Colin rang me from work one day, asking me if I had plans for next Sunday, I asked, "I can't think of anything, why?"

"Well keep it free," he said, "because we're getting married."

♦

I did warn Colin that day that my life was not an easy one, as things just seemed to happen. "Don't expect it to be like a pleasant merry-go-round. It's more like a roller coaster ride," I said, hoping that he might have second thoughts. He said that it was okay, that it would be fun.

And so I became Denise Grant.

Having led a life-to-date that was characterised by traumatic events since my childhood and without ever been granted the opportunity to thoroughly process this trauma, let alone have anyone pause and check-in to see how I was coping, meant I had developed an expert ability to minimise situations and the impact they had on me, regardless of how stressful they were. This enabled me to keep going, to keep holding up against hardship and the emotional turmoil that came with my second marriage. But how much can one person take? How long would it be until I buckled at the seams? I'd reached many thresholds of 'not coping' already, yet as circumstances would have it, I just kept soldiering on.

But there was a tipping point. 1993 was the year that things came to a head. I was not the only one struggling at the time and what occurred was perhaps the last of major events that I and my team of alters could bear to witness.

My mother and David had taken a trip around Australia so I automatically filled the parentified role while they were away. My sister, Kerrie, was now married and the youngest of us all, and Myra had recently separated from her husband. She was on a diet of Valium to combat the depression and anxiety brewing within her. I was keeping in touch with her more often than usual via the phone.

On one particular day I called to check on her, to which she responded, "Don't worry about me, DeeDee." I instinctively knew something was up. She had been spending a lot of time in bed and seemed very calm, not wanting to talk with me much and drifting off during our conversations.

I had a strong urge to go and visit her in Frankston and asked Colin and Kerrie to come with me. This gut-wrenching feeling inside me was urging me to go and be with her, it would not subside. I didn't care if I appeared to be overly dramatic.

When I arrived I found Myra curled up in her bed in a ball under her doona, She was not unlike a hibernating little creature, unmoving, with an air of peace surrounding. I'll never forget how eerily still the scene was. When I probed her to talk, she so was groggy and calm.

"Just go away, DeeDee, this is what I want."

I switched to my default state of panic, however this time it was a different state of affairs because there was someone else involved. Tension and inner conflict erupted inside my mind as I fretted over what to do.

Kerrie soon arrived with her husband, Mark, and we discussed the likelihood that Myra had taken an overdose, as the cause of her groggy state of consciousness Kerrie pottered about making cups of tea while I pondered what needed to happen next. I figured that she was not going to die and hadn't taken more tablets since I'd arrived, but that she could not be left alone from here-on-in. I feared that if we left, she would retrieve a stash of drugs she'd hidden somewhere that none of us knew about. I was determined to not let that happen. When Colin arrived and I relayed the situation to him, he agreed that she was clearly suicidal and extremely vulnerable.

I'm not sure who I rang first, but I got on the phone in an effort to find a sensible solution to the predicament. I could not seem to get anyone to come out and help us until she had been assessed, and to find someone available to assess her was becoming near impossible! So I made the executive decision to drive her to the psychiatric hospital in Frankston, based on the logic that she would be safe there and get an assessment. Kerrie was frightened, Mark did as he was told and Colin was put to task getting Myra in the car. She was literally screaming, biting and kicking both he and Mark like a wildling as they tried to settle her onto the back seat.

By now, Kerrie was crying, and Myra was abusing me. My feelings were so mixed up – I felt as though I was treating her like an animal but I just wanted her to be safe and alive. When we arrived at the hospital only a couple of hours before midnight, bystanders looked on as Myra continued raving like a banshee. One minute she was kicking and biting, the next, giggling and ranting on about it all being a mistake. She hurled filthy words of abuse at me. I wanted to protect her from all the judgemental stares.

"She is going to hate you for this," Kerrie said.

I momentarily wanted to take her home but I had to be strong. We had to get through this. I turned to coffee and cigarettes to get me through the night. By 5am we finally received confirmation from the nurses that yes, she was suicidal and was to be admitted to Larundel Mental Asylum. I signed the forms and felt so guilty for doing it, as though I had completely let my sister down, even though I was trying to do the right thing.

'You did the right thing,' Logical One assured me.

'But what if you had just waited until tomorrow. Maybe she wouldn't have done it?' Poppet chimed in.

I had the psychiatrist's approval to back me.

"I hate you, DeeDee!" my sister yelled from the ambulance after she tried to entice the driver with a head job if he were to drive her home.

I apologised to the driver, who said, "Don't worry love, we get it all the time."

I watched them drive off into the light off dawn.

♦

We later learned that Myra had been suffering from Borderline Personality Disorder, and she was prescribed a lowering daily dose of continued diet of Valium. Her psychiatrist noted that it was such a complicated condition that it could be difficult to find someone in the public sector to treat her. How to find appropriate professional support seemed such a daunting decision to make on my own; I wondered what to tell my mum and David.

'Don't spoil their holiday,' begged Poppet.
'What can they do anyway?' asked Logical One.
'But she is their daughter,' reminded Spiritual One.

"I have had Myra committed," was along the lines of what I said to them, and they returned home early from their holiday, unimpressed. I did not receive any thank you or gesture of gratitude for potentially saving Myra's life. It was more a case of having over-reacted. Myra now wore a 'label' and had been 'looking for attention', my mother explained in her most patronising of tones. The goal had been achieved – to spoil their holiday – but I felt I was the naughty child for making this so.

It is difficult for me to articulate exactly what I felt at the time on an emotional level having been blamed for spoiling Mum and David's trip *and* having my sister unnecessarily committed. The breadth of emotional landscape was too wide for me to navigate and besides, no one even enquired as to how I felt. This set of circumstances was the perfect recipe for my well-honed technique of minimising the event and its associated emotions, and aptly sweeping the entirety of the traumatic drama beneath the carpet. It was to be considered just another 'hiccup', nary making an impression upon my resilient spirit. I simply dealt with it. I got over it. I moved on. Acknowledging the impact of what had happened was not an option. Instead, I suppressed all my feelings and trivialised the whole shebang, retreating even further into my *nothingness* and the departure from reality I could achieve from there.

When Myra had another depressive episode some time later, my mother said, "Maybe you should have let her go,

Denise? It may have been easier all around." The flashing rays of guilt that was so indicative of the dynamic with my mother further weighed me down and my sense of failure became more cemented as a truth.

It was a late-night argument with Colin that later tipped me over the edge. My alters took over with rage and vengefulness towards him, and all the 'craziness' I exhibited (that I have no recollection of) drove him to find me a new psychiatrist. This time, would it be different? Or would it be the same? Just another doctor, another medication, a diagnoses with a slightly different name. I did wonder...

♦

My second marriage was on the rocks. I seemed to have reached a psychiatric dead-end. It was 1999. I felt vulnerable, empty; lost in distortions of time, memory, and inner-voice confusion. Desperate to get through this, I decided breeding rabbits might help. Surely they'd be less heartbreaking than dogs. I was holding down a job for an accounts team in the city. The trains no longer rattled, and it was during this time that I was referred by my doctor to see a psychologist – the therapist who finally, *correctly*, diagnosed me.

I had gone to see Dr Lee off the back end of another tiff with Colin. I was at a loose end as to what to do with the unbearable inner state of being the fight had triggered, so the receptionist gave me the first appointment of the next morning.

When I entered his room, I recall sobbing uncontrollably after he asked what he could do for me.

"I can't take it anymore!" I blubbered.

In a discombobulated manner, I prattled on about fighting with Colin over making cups of coffee for our kids. All my alters were chiming in with their versions of the story, and possibly other stories too, who knows! All I recall is feeling silly, with no idea what I was doing at the appointment and watched him thumb through the index of a book to retrieve a phone number. He wrote me a referral to a psychologist, and I followed his instructions to make an appointment .

I met with Annabel on an April autumn day for a 4:30pm appointment. Colin showed up for support. It was the beginning of the end of my second marriage, and an end to the psychological journey I had been on all my life, yet this time, with the promise of a new beginning.

It was Annabel who described me as a 'Functioning Multiple' and formally diagnosed me with Dissociative Identity Disorder. Yes, I think I was normal for most of the time but these lapses and losses, relentless confusion, the *Unknown Friends Within*, that was definitely part of me too.

During my final years with Colin, I had many mixed emotions flooding through me that I began to unpack through therapy with Annabel, alongside a thorough exploration of my past. I was finally being offered a safe space to look at it *all* and a diagnoses to give it context. I felt like a complete failure in life and wasn't coping very well but her appointments were propping me up. There continued to be arguments at home, and I would plead with my children to behave, to keep the peace.

My head was still throbbing with pain and exhaustion.

I recall one day – an appointment with Annabel day – when I was standing on the corner of two inner-city streets, with no explanation as to why I was there. I had no idea of how I came to this point – this corner, this place, this life. Nor did I know which was the way back to work. I panicked. Momentarily forgetting about my alters, all I knew I was a very long way from the office. I just stood there watching trams go past, reading the destinations on them to trace my way back. I had left the office at 12:30pm but now, when I checked my watch, it was 4pm. Life continued to be filled with these episodic black-outs but at least I now had someone to talk them through with. Someone I trusted, who showed me their genuine care.

I discovered a new strategy of removing myself from stressful situations, just to keep my head above water. One day, when I thought my head was about to explode, I got into my car and kept driving. When I eventually stopped, I gathered up a blanket from out of my car and lay on it. I attempted to quieten the noises in my head but I must have dropped off asleep. The next thing I recognised was the sound of soft breathing hovering above me. I woke up, rolled over and came face-to-face with a beautiful cow. She was standing over me as we both wondered, what are *you* doing here?

I returned home to my family who didn't notice me when I got back. Corey and Jodie were stationed in their rooms. Colin was mowing the lawns. I started cooking tea, deciding to keep my meeting with the cow to myself. I wondered if she had told her family about me or if it was our little secret?

How silly are the thoughts in my head. I smiled to myself, knowing that this was the kind of story that would make Isobella happy. She would understand. And so would Annabel.

PART THREE

Our Story

I found it awfully hard to tell my family and friends about my diagnoses, and I must admit, I was hurt by some of their reactions. For the most part though, I received a lot of support.

My daughter's reaction was a surprise to me. She just burst into tears. "Oh, Mum, I just thought you were a cold-hearted bitch. You never seemed to be there for me," she said. In hindsight, I understood what she was referring to. When I would escape to my *nothing* place, I was unaware of the things that were going on around me. Clearly this impacted her significantly and I felt immensely guilty about it but at least Jodie and I could now start discussing the reasons for my behaviour; she realised that it was never intentional and that I had always loved her.

Corey, on the other hand, was more concerned about what it all meant for now. His first words to me were, "Gee, Mum, does that mean you are going to be one of those people who go around talking to themselves?"

"Oh, for goodness sake, of course not!" I chuckled.

"Do you not feel cheated out of a life?" he ventured on with.

"No, not really," I replied. "I thought everyone was like me."

I realised that this was all meant to be. It is not what happens to you that matters, it is how you deal with it. I have many times thanked Spiritual One who reminds me of this so very often. As Corey and I discussed my experience further, he asked if it was a bit like the television show *Herman's Head*, which seemed to be the closest I could ever have likened it to something. This seemed to help him wrap his own head around my condition.

My closest friends, Ray and Carmel, seemed to be delighted. Carmel said it was such a relief to them to know what was really going on for me. She said that they had probably already met my other personalities. Their response warmed my heart as they were so accepting.

"It just explains so much," Carmel said. "We would often go home after being with you and comment on how differently you had been acting but we just accepted that that was just you – just a little bit strange!" she said lovingly.

I lost a lot of friends during that time. I wondered whether they thought I was just making it all up or looking for attention or perhaps, did not know how to deal with it. But my biggest disappointment was my family, who I have now been estranged from since early 2001. It seems my diagnoses was just too much for them to accept.

After telling my mother, it seemed to have fallen on deaf ears. Any conversation I had with her was always the same. She would ask how I was, I would try and explain, and then she'd cut me short by telling me about things that were happening in her life.

"Did I tell you how I got closest to the pin in my last game of golf?" or "Poor David, he's been working so hard lately. You know what he's like, he never stops," she'd prattle on.

Not once did she ask about my sessions with Annabel, yet I'd hear all about her Merna, her dislocated shoulder, her woes.

"It's just not like Merna," she announced one interrupted moment on the phone. "She actually cried on the phone. First time she has ever done that. It's not fair, is it?"

"No, it's not fair," I weakly agreed, wishing I had the strength to just put down the phone, but before I could do so she had started on about Judy.

"I must go and see her. Poor Judy had to go into hospital and is being operated on to have her lymph glands removed from under her arm! She may have to have a mastectomy!"

At which point, Logical One burst forth in an attempt to take charge of the conversation with little tact. "Have you said anything to David about my problem yet?" Logical One asked.

"Ah, yes, I have. Not that he really understands it all."

"What did he say?"

"Nothing really. He is genuinely concerned about you but cannot imagine what it must be like. He thinks a lot. I see him staring out the window sometimes and I ask him what he is thinking about it. He just says, nothing."

Like hell he's not! I think.

"But that's just like him, isn't it? Keeps it all bottled up. I know he is worried about you but feels helpless, I guess."

Oh, Mum, if only you knew! I seem to get some sense of

satisfaction out of this. I wonder whether he's worried about the consequences if I should say anything. I let him squirm but he may have forgotten and may not even be thinking anything. I hope to myself it's the first option and have come to terms with how I'm to handle it.

'*Later*,' Logical One insisted. '*We will revisit this as I am not sure.*'

♦

I finally ended the conversation with Mum by saying I must go and take a shower as I have an appointment with Dr Lee about my headaches.

"Ring me when you get back, darling, 'cos I do worry about you," she said. "See what Dr Lee says and be guided by him."

There's a hint that 'all this other stuff' can be dealt with by him in the undercurrent of what she said; that he will 'know what to do.'

'*Oh well, she means well,*' Spiritual One reminded me. '*You are one of her little chicks that has left the nest and she just can't let you go.*'

'*What a load of codswallop. She's just a very manipulating woman and I fear she does not want the past to be revisited,*' warned Janice.

♦

Dr Lee prescribed me antibiotics for my sinus, panadeine for the pain and Xanax for the tension. Every time Mum would phone, I felt helpless. On and on she would go and I could feel myself wanting to scream down the line, wanting her to just hang up. My headaches would then flare to peak at such unbearable pain, and I wanted to vomit. Why couldn't she just listen to me for once? I could not go on like this. I felt abandoned at a time when I wanted my mum to listen to me and support me but instead, she just shut me out.

By this time, I was now on a Disability Support Pension and was deemed unfit for work. Dr Lee thought it was more appropriate to say I suffered from panic attacks and anxiety. These were definitely symptoms of my condition but my real diagnoses, Dissociative Identity Disorder, was not widely known or understood. To sustain my pension, my routine involved going to the doctor once a fortnight to get a certificate to cover me for two weeks, then off to Centrelink to get my pension for another fortnightly payment. It all felt so demeaning and one day I just broke down in the company of my Centrelink support person. I was crying and blubbering, so she called for someone while I wept and they ushered me into a private room.

Slowly I calmed myself down but was visibly distressed. When one of the women asked me what the matter was, I told her about my true diagnoses. "It is so awful, and I feel like such a failure," I sobbed. We talked for quite some time, and she tried to reassure me. She seemed genuinely interested in what I was saying. I left feeling somewhat lighter having shared some of the load I was carrying.

A couple of days had passed, and I received a phone call from her.

"I have spoken to my manager about you and she in turn has spoken to our Canberra office, to get permission for you to come along to our head office in Melbourne," she said.

"Oh, okay. But why?" I asked, fearing the worst.

"We were wondering if you would feel comfortable about coming in and talking to some of our support workers to give them a better understanding of what you're going through."

I certainly didn't have a problem with that and took down the details of when and where to meet them.

A few weeks later, I attended the meeting and when I arrived I was a little taken aback by the amount of people in the room. Many were not even from Centrelink. There were doctors, psychologists, and other professionals in the medical field. I don't quite recall what I talked about but I felt extremely comfortable in their presence. It was both a comfort and a relief to know they were so interested in what I had to say. A week after my talk, I got another call from Centrelink.

"Sorry to bother you, Denise," said the voice down the phone, "but one of the doctors who attended your talk last week, went home and told his wife about you. She has asked if you'd be available to do an interview. She is studying journalism and is interested in your story for an assignment."

I didn't mind in the slightest and made arrangements for the interview to go ahead. We agreed that she could come to my place for an informal chat. It turned out to be a lovely encounter and I felt very comfortable discussing my experiences with her. Being seen, heard and acknowledged by someone who was not judging me for my condition was having a positive impact on my wellbeing and was at such strong contrast to the disinterest of my mother.

Down the track when the journalist had completed her assignment, she sent me an email to thank me for my contribution. It read:

Hi Denise,

I hope this finds you well. I just wanted to let you know that I got my marks back for our article this week. It received a high distinction – 95 out of 100. My best mark yet! Take care and thank you. (Read the article in full in the reference section of this book.)

After this experience, I *never* had to submit another Medical Certificate to Centrelink ever again. I continued to receive my pension and my contribution of sharing my story more widely, proved to be very worthwhile.

♦

One morning I woke up, grabbed the phone and rang Jodie. "I'm going to see Mum and make her listen to me," I said.

It was time to tell her about David. It was time to get this all off my chest. It was time to surrender the burden I'd been carrying and that continued to make me sick. Perhaps then, she would understand.

"Oh God, Mum, are you sure?" Jodie said.

"I have to, Jodie. I have kept this bottled up for so long, trying to protect her. Where is she when I need her? Where is she when I need her to help me?"

"I am coming with you," Jodie said adamantly.

I was so grateful.

I also rang Myra and Kerrie who were both eager to support me but they themselves didn't really know the extent of what I was about to expose. We arranged to meet at a park beforehand for a debrief. Once we had all gathered in the car park, I explained to my sisters about David. Even though they were shocked, I wasn't expecting them to react the way that they did.

It was Kerrie who said, "We knew there was something going on."

"Yes," Myra concurred.

"Why?" I asked. "What do you mean?"

They went on to tell me about a day they were on the upstairs balcony, looking down and watching Mum, David, Ian and me. We had been swimming in the pool and then took photos of each other with the new polaroid camera.

"So, big deal!" I exclaimed.

"No, DeeDee. You were all laughing and taking pictures down the front of each other's bathers. We thought it was all a bit sick, really."

I had no recollection of that day and to be honest, it was more than a bit sick – it was bloody disgusting!

"Didn't Mum try to stop it?" I enquired.

"No, she was laughing and taking photos as well," they explained.

Other occasions were mentioned included the many parties hosted at our home. I had no idea what they were talking about and didn't want to know any more details. I didn't have the capacity to process it and wanted to confront my mother more than ever.

When we arrived at her house, she welcomed us by saying she was pleased to see us and went and put on the kettle.

"No, Mum. I need to talk to you now," I demanded.

One of the other's told her to sit down, that what I was about to share could come as a shock. I was single-pointedly focussed on voicing my truth.

My memory of what came next is very blurry, but I know I managed to tell Mum about the awful abuse David had committed over the years when I was a child. I recall being unable to look at her as I spoke for fear of bursting into tears. Myra, Kerrie and Jodie helped me out by explaining some of the gaps in my story and when it was all said and done, I couldn't believe I had actually let the cat out of the bag. My stomach was tied up in knots and I wanted to flee. Mum sat silent, motionless. I almost felt sorry for her. Why had I done it?

Then David walked in and by now, I was sinking into a world of pain. My head was throbbing relentlessly, the worst of its kind. I wanted to throw up everywhere; my hands were sweating, and I could feel a film of clamminess take over my whole body while he casually wandered into the room, looking at us.

Mum turned to welcome him. "Come and sit down, darling. We're just having a chat. Do you know what it might be about?" she asked.

"I think so," was all he muttered.

"So, is any of it true?"

"Well, yes," he admitted. "But she enjoyed it!"

What?! I was 11 years old! Only a little girl!

I thought that in that pivotal moment I disappeared somewhere else but according to Jodie, all of my personalities came out in one hit. Some were crying, others were screaming. Some screeched obscenities. Jodie recounts the display as unbelievable to witness. The I went on to directly abuse him with very unpleasant language. The rage

I felt and expressed knew no boundaries; on and on I went, screaming and yelling, until Jodie decided it was time to go.

All I remember her saying was, "Come on, Mum. I think it's time to take you home."

I'm grateful Jodie took charge. She could see I was in a world of pain and didn't really know what would happen if she hadn't stepped in. Me and my personalities had lost all sense of control. I remember asking her in the car, "Did I really do it?"

"Boy, did you ever!" she replied. We both laughed hysterically.

"If I ever needed any proof of your *others*, I certainly got it then, Mum."

When we got home, she made me go to bed and rest, giving me one of my magic tablets. I slowly drifted off to sleep, bewildered at what had taken place and now feeling safe and supported.

When I woke up the next morning, Corey came rushing in, telling me to put on the TV. I did as he instructed and couldn't quite comprehend, at first, what was happening. Planes were flying into buildings, bursting into fire while the Twin Towers in America crumbled like a stack of cards. It was like the end of the world. People were running for their lives across the streets and the news readers fought back their tears. It was unbelievable. Utter chaos and panic took over with no one able to explain what was happening.

"Well, I never," was all I could say in disbelief. "I dropped a bomb yesterday and now this," and because of the difference in date and time, it had all happened on the same day.

September 11th, 2001.

♦

Earlier that year on the April 17th, my first grandchild, Michael, was born. Witnessing Jodie become a mother brought me so much joy, and Michael's presence in my life, especially during this time of change, relieved me of focussing too much on my condition and instead on embracing my extended family.

However, his first birthday seemed to trigger a flood of mixed feelings on my part. It was a noteworthy experience and took a great deal of energy to contain my other personalities, since it involved gathering everyone together. The younger alters were fearful, some just didn't want to attend and others, well, I think they went into hiding.

Jodie invited us to meet at the picnic grounds at Cardinia Dam, which I felt was ideal since we could be outdoors in nature rather than confined to four walls in a house. We were all there, Mum and David, Jodie and Corey, Jodie's friends, my sisters and their children, along with Ray and Carmel too. They even bought their daughters, Leanne and Cathy, along with Ray and Carmel's grandson Bayley. It was indeed, a large family gathering and I had good reason for my social anxiety to become exacerbated in the lead up. Seeing Mum and David in a public setting made me very nervous.

I felt I wasn't really present to the experience; I kind of shut down, to begin with, which is all I ever knew to do under these types of circumstances. I could snap out of it when playing with Michael or talking with Ray and Carmel, and be warm and present to their company, however in general, I avoided connecting with anyone else. At one point I went for a walk with Kerrie's daughter, Jacyln, who was five years old and Ray and Carmel's grandson Bayley, who was three. We went to see the kangaroos and it was a situation I felt comfortable in and grounded. I was free, calm and content, then all of a sudden Ray appeared beside me.

"Just keep walking," he said. "You've got company behind you."

I followed his instruction but glanced back to see Mum and David, among a few others, following closely behind me. "Shit, Ray," I said. "What do I do?" I started giggling, then I became trapped within a fit of giggles! "'You always find the funny side, don't you, Mizzy?"

Ray chuckled which kept things light and said, "Come on, just keep walking. I hope we're heading in the direction of home!"

As luck would have it, a small bridge appeared over the creek ahead of us, so we hurried across it to distance ourselves from the group. Jaclyn kept calling back to the others to hurry up while I tried to hush her to keep walking or the kangaroos would be frightened.

It was absurd really, Ray with his grandson, me with my niece, all trudging through the undergrowth in search for elusive roos. Isobella found it delightful playing along with the children, as though we were on a big adventure. In a sense, we were on a mission trying to lose the others and find sanctuary as quickly as possible. When we arrived back at the picnic grounds we were safe, able to find our own space while others gathered and mingled amongst each other. It was not until after the cake came out and we all sang happy birthday to Michael that the crowd slowly dissipated, and my mother found an in-road to appear out of nowhere and approach me.

I froze. Then before I could even think about what to do next, we were embracing. I felt her sincere efforts in that moment, in her hug, to try and make everything better. She was doing her best in that moment to reach out and connect.

"Don't be a stranger," she whispered in my ear. "We are always here for you, just pick up the phone."

"I can't do that," I said blankly, almost as a knee-jerk response to her rapid move and pressed on to explain that things could never go back to normal nor back to how they were before.

I took the opportunity to tell her how upset I was about her wanting me to put the guys back in a Pandora's Box. How, when she asked why I hadn't told her about David, that all I could manage to say was that I felt it would have upset her too much. That with the help of my *Unknown Friends Within*, I had survived. Yet I was now feeling helpless about what my life had come to.

"We all feel like that sometimes," she said.

She really didn't understand what I was trying to say. She really had no idea or didn't want to know what my life had been like. "But no, Mum. I am only now accepting the fact that I have DID and that all these things really did happen to me."

"I don't know how to help you," she said and while she spoke, I picked up on a slight tremor in her voice.

If only I could bring myself to say that it was okay, to not worry about me, that everything would be all right; I knew she would have eventually felt better. But this, I could not do.

I continued to explain to her how I felt, however, I do not remember the details of what I said. The parts that stood out most were when I told her about Dr Joe C and how my brain was wired differently – clinically, not emotionally – and how I would never forget what David had done.

"It was wrong, Mum, so very wrong. He should never have done that to me."

"It was despicable what he did to you," she agreed. "And I don't like being alone with him and he knows it! I also know our family, as we knew it, has gone," she added. "But hey, that's life I guess."

She then went on to ask, or should I say rather, stated the fact: "Does that mean my life has been nothing but a lie?"

Hello! I thought to myself. *Your life? What about mine?!*

Guilt. Remorse. My fault. They all charged in at that precise moment. I couldn't handle carrying another load and I felt great anger towards her. I realise now that somewhere in her mind she was saying, *Poor me. Why me?* like a martyr.

And even though I understood the little voice of Isobella pierced through the surface to say, "Yes, but what about me, Mummy?"

For perhaps, if she had just expressed to *me* an ounce of compassion, it would have made the world of difference. Perhaps she did feel sorry for me and has never quite known how to say it or may never even know that that is what I need to hear.

'Now who's being a martyr?' remarked Mizzy.

With that emotionally charged, awkward but important conversation out of the way, I returned to the tail-end of the picnic and jumped in to help Jodie pack up what was left behind. She certainly had had her fair share of drinks at the celebration, so Mark, Rodney and I stayed back to help her clean up. When it was my turn to leave after feeling quite drained from the events of the day, Jodie and her friends were still at the table drinking wine merrily. It was a memorable first birthday for Michael indeed, for so many varied reasons, new and old. I spent the last minutes carrying and cuddling Michael, singing gently to him while he chattered back.

A weight had been lifted from my shoulders, which was already noticeable while I coddled my grandson. I felt at peace and proud to be a grandmother too. The panoramic views around Cardinia Dam had a palpable majesty about them, endowing grace and beauty across the open fields and thick tree canopy. The kangaroos, now spared the maddening picnic crowds, were free to roam and dine on the grass as the sun set behind them. I could think of nowhere I'd rather be than there, in that precious, *Magic Moment*.

Nature embraced both Michael and I as we left the tracks to get closer to the roos, who were unperturbed by our presence. All seemed well in my world; nothing else mattered. It was Michael, me, the kangaroos, the sunset. So simple, yet boy was my spirit soaring. Michael was delighting in the environment, pointing and pursing his lips, looking at the wildlife then back at me to ensure I was looking also. I found it extremely difficult to pull us away from this moment of peace and pleasure, but the chill of the night was settling in and I knew it was time to turn back. I sang softly to him and his weary eyes as we made our way back to Jodie.

"Micky moo, Micky moo saw and loved the kangaroo,' I sang. We took our time returning. I had survived another day.

♦

I now had my diagnoses and a context in which I could understand the often times chaotic realms of my inner-world, and while this was a positive breakthrough on my life journey, it didn't quite temper my alters. It was more a case of learning to live with them, love them and function in the world, and in a way, try and move on from the debilitating years of the impact of my trauma. It was helpful that other people could understand me better and I became more accepting of the situations I found myself in because of my multiple personalities.

Like the hit and run incident that seemingly came out of nowhere. I'll never forget that! I had received notice via an email from Mum and David that they had sold another of their investment properties, also in Cheltenham. They had put aside some of the money to give to me. They were away at the time, and I wanted to avoid seeing them, so there was some urgency in picking up the cash before they returned. My window was slim.

I threw on some shoes, grabbed my bag and was off. During the long drive to their house, I noticed mixed feelings arising the closer I came to their vicinity. I felt sneaky, scared, anxious. What if they arrived when I was there? My alters became very active at the time; it seemed everyone had something to say.

'*So what if they arrive? You're not doing anything wrong,*' said Quassie, who was surprisingly very level-headed about the matter.

But Poppet could not be appeased. '*What are they thinking about us?*'

'*Hey! Hang on! You didn't ask for the bloody money anyway,*' Mizzy pointed out.

'Yes, but I feel naughty,' replied Poppet.

'Look, you have never asked them for anything and they offered, didn't they?' reasoned Quassie.

'I guess so,' was my response, but why was I so nervous? I wished I wasn't doing this, I thought to myself when I pulled up in their driveway. My heart was racing.

'If their car is there, keep driving,' instructed Logical One.

'And what? Go straight to Nana's,' asked Poppet.

'Yes, that's the trick!' said Mizzy.

I was very relieved to find that no one was home. Yet I also felt very sick. The guys were talking at me all at once. My mouth had turned dry, my pulse was racing, and my head throbbed. I put the car in park mode, jumped out, quickly opened the meter box, and there it was. A green envelope! 'To Denise, love from David,' it said.

I stared at the handwriting. *How dare he!*

A mixture of paralysis and a strong sickly stirring came over me. I couldn't take my eyes off the envelope when all for a sudden I was interrupted by a loud *crunch* sound.

Fuck! What had I done? I snapped back to the present moment and discovered myself standing in the middle of the road at the bottom of the driveway. I had hit the brick letterbox with my car, and it had crumbled onto the pavement, bricks strewn everywhere. I still held my gaze on the envelope but as I lifted my eyes to look around it became apparent that I had backed down the driveway and for the life of me, could not remember doing it.

'You didn't do it, I did!' said Mizzy, sounding rather proud of herself.

'Now you've done it,' said Poppet, upset. *'I knew no good*

would come of this and now Mummy will be so cross.'

'I wasn't meant to have that money. Now I will have to use it to get my car fixed. Sod it!' said Janice.

'Quick, run!' said Poppet.

'Just get out of here. They may come back,' ordered Poppet.

I was panic-stricken. I couldn't believe what had just happened and wanted to escape the scene.

'Oh, for goodness sake, just get out of here! Ring them later!' said Logical One.

'And say what? Thanks for the money. Sorry about the letterbox?' giggled Mizzy.

My head was spinning with all the different voices spinning around me. The alters were now all talking at once and I could recognise it as noise which was the cause of my headaches.

'What will they say? Oh, why had I come down? All for the bloody money. I am a bad girl.'

'Just go round to Nana's. Move it. Worry about it later,' insisted Logical One.

And that is what I did. As I arrived at Nana's it was raining and the details of what had transpired felt surreal.

'Don't say anything, please. They won't know,' said Isobella. *'Knowing our luck, a neighbour would have seen what happened and they would tell them,'* she went on.

'Just pretend you didn't notice,' was Mizzy's solution.

'Yeah, good one,' I said. *'What about my car?'*

Before going inside to see Nana, I did a quick check of my car. There was no major damage. Some paint had been scratched off but that was all. I started to giggle with relief along with Poppet and Mizzy by my side.

'See, they will never know, will they?' Isobella said hopefully.

I decided to be hopeful too. This was not the first time me and my alters had caused innocent trouble and I was still alive to tell the many tales.

♦

Settling in at Nana's, sipping tea and catching up, the hit and run incident became a far and distant memory. Nana was pleased to see me as I was her. I always felt a cosy safety in her presence. She enquired as to whether I had gone to see my family on Mother's Day.

"I was in Mildura, Nana," I said.

"Oh, I see," she said but my Nana was not stupid. I could see that she was picking up on something; she had *that look* and pressed on with the questions.

"Gerry says he doesn't blame you for keeping your distance from the family. He can only take your mother for so long, then he has had enough. Is that why you don't see them anymore?"

Gerry was my uncle. It was nice to know he shared the same sentiments but my experience of my mother was incomparable. "Not really, Nana," I said.

"You are very much like me. We both like our independence but I think your mother is puzzled by it all. I ask her how you are but she never seems to know. Oh well, perhaps one day it will get better."

'See,' Mizzy pointed out, *'She's not giving up'.*

Then it was as though Nana had overheard Mizzy and went on to say she was worried about me and hoped I was doing okay. Time seemed to stand still. I couldn't just sit there.

'Tell her, go on,' Mizzy said.

'I can't. What would mum say?' I felt so anxious and could feel Poppet drawing in close.

'This is your Nana. Sod your mum. Just don't tell her about David,' instructed Janice.

Before I could stop myself, I found myself telling Nana all about my alters. It just sort of spilled out everywhere in the comfort of my Nana's listening ear and I explained to her that the reason Mum and I were so distant was because Mum could not accept them as part of my life; as part of who I was.

"Well I never!" she said. "What's wrong with your mother?"

"Oh, I don't know," I sighed. "I guess it really is just a bit unbelievable, Nana."

"Well, how did it start?" she enquired.

I explained to her the impact my father's death had had on me, how it was after then that I shut myself off from the pain. That I had never properly dealt with it nor healed and that dissociating myself from the pain by introducing my alters into my world was how my brain learnt to cope.

Nana then guided the conversation back to when I was a little girl when we used to share a room together. We both fondly recalled our late nights up together, talking and chattering away. "You didn't want your mum to marry David, did you?" she said.

I used to keep Nana awake for hours, she went on to say, with the need to talk and express myself. And Nana, like now, was always there for me, lovingly bearing witness to it all.

"Right when I thought you were about to settle down and fall asleep, out would come the nail polish, at midnight! You would sit there filing away and painting your nails, as if there was nothing wrong."

Together we laughed and chatted on her sofa for what felt like hours. She didn't seem to think I was stupid. She seemed to understand, for she too had led a colourful life marked by many challenges.

"I often wonder how I survived," she remarked. "No normal person would have done half as much as I did. And when I think of all the strife I would get myself into, I would find myself thinking it was all meant to be. I agree with you – there is a plan. I often thought I was going mad and I wonder what all those old dears (fellow residents in her retirement home) would say if they knew what I had been up to. Sometimes it can all get a bit too much and I would have to stop and listen to my tapes for about half an hour just to shut off." She was referring to her talking books. How well I understood those feelings.

"You know, I often wonder who your mother takes after," she went on. "I can't figure her out at times, although she was always there for me and she does a lot for me but I can't talk to her like I can with you. She treats me like a child sometimes. She can be so bossy. But I guess she means well."

"I know, Nana, but this time I cannot do as she wishes. I cannot put my guys in a box and pretend they don't exist, not even for her."

"Well, I'll tell you something now," she said. "About two months ago it started. Every so often I would be doing something, and a voice would tell me to 'do it later' or 'you don't really need to do that'. And it startled me. I thought I might be going mad. You know, old age catching up with me but it was beginning to annoy me. What right did it have to tell me what I could or could not do?" And she laughed again. "I did tell your mother but she just swept it aside by saying that yes, I was going mad and jokingly changed the subject. She didn't want to talk about it."

'No imagination!' piped up Mizzy before I could stop her.

The alters, Nana and I, we all started laughing. How easy it was to be with my Nana and how special it felt knowing that she, too, felt at ease talking to me.

'Your mother will kill you is she finds out about this,' Poppet said to me, who was now feeling very guilty. *'How dare you worry your Nana with all this.'*

'But hey, hang on a minute!' interrupted Mizzy. *'It's all in good fun and we haven't said anything about David. Besides, Nana is being heard and we've had a hearty, harmless giggle. She still has her wits about her. Why must we wrap her up in cotton wool?'* asked Mizzy, who couldn't fathom what the big deal was.

'It will keep her awake at night worrying about it,' said Poppet, *'and you know Mum won't like it.'*

'Hell's bells!' exclaimed Mizzy. *'It will give her something to think about? So what! It will give her time out from being bored.'*

Again, it was as though Nana knew what was being said between us all despite being unable to hear the actual voices. She began ushering me on my way, saying, "Well, it's been lovely, Deneez but we are having tea soon and I really think I need half an hour of tapes before then. We are such a pair, you and I. You've certainly given me something to think about."

I did love the way she pronounced my name *Deneez.*

We hugged and upon parting, she said, "God bless. Take care. I'm going to have it out with that voice tonight. I'm going to ask him who he is," and we both broke out into laughter.

"Good luck," I said. "I can only hope he's the only one who

answers you."

"Oh my giddy aunt," she said laughing. "So do I!" She disappeared inside before I had even reached my car.

'Well, you've done it now!' Mizzy remarked mischievously.

Poppet grew more anxious. *'I am a naughty girl. Mummy said she would kill me if I worried Nana with all this.'*

'Sod her again! We didn't drop David in the shit, so what's the problem?' You've done it now!' said Mizzy.

It was Spiritual One who then stepped in to take control of the situation brewing. *'Remember your nana's words. There is a plan. Think of her more as another soul. It was all meant to be. She is not just your nana. Your paths on this life journey have a much deeper connection, so with this in mind, feel no guilt. It was part of the plan.'*

'OMG, you are so right. Thank you Spiritual One,' I said, feeling gladdened by the reminder. If only I could draw on her wise words more often and hold that thought, I would feel less anxious and panic-stricken. How to get the others to believe her too, was the hard part.

As I was driving home, I remembered the money and the brick letterbox. Then memory hit me suddenly so I had to pull over to gather myself. I pulled out the envelope to take another look at it.

'No wonder I had smashed down the letterbox,' said Mizzy.

I re-read the writing, *To Denise, Lots of love, David*, slowly recognising that it was in my mother's handwriting.

Janice screamed inside me. I started up the car again. I just wanted to get home as soon as possible. It all seemed so surreal.

When I arrived home, I told Corey everything, who said,

"Oh well. Accidents do happen. Are you going to offer to pay for it?"

'Sod off!' said Mizzy. *'It's not like we did it on purpose.'*

I rang Jodie to ask for her advice.

"You had better tell them somehow," she said, "or they'll think it was me."

And then I started laughing. I couldn't help it. I laughed so much, I became hysterical. The more we discussed the incident the more the laughter became uncontrollable. I was in pain, I was laughing so much. I could barely breathe. Tears were rolling down my face, at which point I started to wail. "Oh God, Jodie, what have I done?"

By this time Jodie was in a similar state as me. Neither of us could stop laughing. She even had to hand the phone to Mark and take a break from the conversation to regain herself, but to no avail. It seemed to make matters worse, and I was in agony from so much laughing!

In the end, I begged to Jodie to hang up.

"No, you hang up!" she insisted and into hysterics we fell again.

She managed to string her final words together, asking if I wanted her to come round. She was getting slightly worried about me verging on hysteria.

"No, it's okay, darling. I'm going to yoga soon," I managed to say. I was gasping, trying to return to my breath.

Eventually we both calmed down. I reassured Jodie of my sanity, as much as I could do so given the broader circumstances. It was a time when laughter really was the best medicine, my yoga mat waiting on the horizon at the end of another hectic day, whereby everyone – yet again – had so much to say. And we could find the humour.

♦

I continued my sessions with Annabel exploring the many layers of myself and my condition, when one day she asked me what I wanted to do for the rest of my life. I replied, "I want to stand on top of a mountain and yell, 'It's okay to have a mental illness!'" Yes, that is what I sincerely wanted to do.

She went on to tell me about Care Ring, a phone counselling service/call centre that took calls from people who were experiencing challenges. Annabel had done work experience with them previously when she was studying psychology and thought I might be interested working at the call centre. She thought it could do me good to start leaving the house a little more too. "Look them up and see what you think," she said. "That's your homework for the week." The idea appealed to me; perhaps it would bring me a sense of purpose.

The following day I called them and was told that there was a Selection Day scheduled for the following Saturday. They asked me if I would be interested in attending. Of course I was and gave them my details. So that was that.

Saturday came and off I went to the selection day.

'What if we don't get selected?' Poppet. The doubts were beginning to take over.

'Don't be silly, of course we will get selected,' said Mizzy.

'Besides, if we don't get selected you have at least given it a go,' encouraged Spiritual One.

'And don't be too disappointed as it has been quite some time since we have even gone to work,' reminded Logical One.

I know they were trying hard to help and give me confidence, but the doubts were still prominent.

My next visit with Annabel was quite funny as she followed up on how I had gone with my homework.

"Good," I said. "My training starts in September, and I am extremely excited about it. I know I can be of some help to others. Where this will lead, heaven only knows!"

"Okay, that is good but which part of *just look them up* didn't you understand?" she asked, with a knowing smile on her face.

"Oh, but when I rang to check them out, they said they were having a Selection Day last Saturday, and you know me, in for a penny and in for a pound. Off I went!"

After attending a Selection Day and overcoming my niggling doubts about returning to work, I quickly moved into a training role. Bill was my support person and we instantly had good rapport. He lightened the load with his jocularity for it was sometimes heavy going. My buttons were being pushed left, right and centre as themes of childhood abuse, neglect, sexual assault and suicide were the main topics of discussion coming through the call centre.

But I pressed on with the task at hand, learning so much every day. I began to feel less isolated and even started to function better on a daily basis. I was exhausted at the end of each day though.

I amazed myself how aptly I fulfilled the training criteria with answers to my practise callers. I'd assume a kind of play-acting role, with words effortlessly rolling off my tongue to the training questions. I sensed things. It was as though I knew what was expected of me, a lot of it deriving from gut instinct and a lot from my personal experience. I noticed a small battle beginning to play-out inside me. How much was

I to reveal about myself? How much was the right amount to share?

Becoming involved with Care Ring brought a sense of belonging and increased self-esteem. I was taking the reins of my own life now, yet one afternoon when Jodie arrived at my home to pick up Corey on the way to seeing my mother, I realised I was still quite vulnerable. My parents, sisters, children, nieces, nephews and my grandson were all gathering together and I was moving further away, so it seemed, catching my train to Care Ring each day and being distanced from family.

I felt alone. And Janice started to taunt me. *'I told you so, lonely and depressed. You have no one to blame but yourself, kiddo. Why do you fight me so?'* she said. *'Give it up. The family is all together now but you chose not to be with them. You were the one who said, "No, I'm not going." So why are you feeling so miserable? Their lives will go on regardless. You are walking away from them; they're not worried about you.'*

When Janice starts, she can be so hurtful. All my pain was being prodded to the surface. There was truth in her bitter words.

"Shut up, all of you." It was my turn to get aggravated now and I could sense my alters paying me some attention. There was debate amongst us on the pros and cons of my life as it was, all the while I was riding the train to work; this racket in my mind brought on a severe headache. I pleaded with them all to stop, to leave me alone and was relieved when the train finally arrived at my station.

I had Care Ring now. I was making a difference, no matter how small. When I got to work, I began to feel more comfortable. Familiar faces showed up and we'd share a chat and a laugh before starting the night shift. I belonged to this community of doing good. After I completed the six months of training, I was given the 9pm–4am shift every Friday. I found it extremely rewarding being able to assist the many callers needing support. Isobella loved our after-work ritual and what took shape was a positive lifestyle around my new role.

'Remember how we used to make sure we had an apple with us when we went to Care Ring,' recalled Isobella.

And I did. We used to stand in Flagstaff Gardens with an apple in hand to feed the possums at the end of our long night shift.

♦

My time at Care Ring lasted 18 months when it started to feel as though the stress of taking so many calls from people who were really struggling, was taking its toll on my own mental health. I was beginning to feel burnt out and the suicidal calls in particular distressed me, for I never really knew the outcomes. This all weighed heavily on me, and I wondered if there was more that I could do, when in reality, I couldn't. The job had served its purpose, however, and Annabel continued to prompt me with ideas as to how to continue leading a healthy, harmonious life. I also had the wisdom of Spiritual One to support me.

'No, my dear, it's time you took some time out. Rebuild your strength,' she said.

And so I turned to my love of animals, which had always bought me comfort and acquired a puppy who I called Beau. He became an unconditionally loving new member of my inner-family, bringing me and my alters so much joy.

Eventually my small animal sanctuary grew to include Beau, my dog, T2 the rabbit, and the Love Birds. Life with all the animals kept me busy. One day I found myself shovelling compost on to the garden to take my mind off Beau who was at the vets being de-sexed. Marm and Jon both encouraged me to get stuck into some gardening as I was fretting about the operation. He survived, of course, and appeared to love me when I picked him up. We had forged a very strong bond.

Continuing gardening with Beau around was awkward as he was such an active puppy and with the rabbit running about, one of them would be digging up wherever I had tended; on and on they went. Beau thought it was a fun game to chase T2 around but this rabbit didn't have the stamina of a puppy and would try and hide in the bushes. One day T2 turned around and bit Beau on the neck! With blood seeping everywhere and clearly in a lot of pain, I ended up taking Beau to the vet and explaining he had been bitten by a rabbit.

The receptionists and the vet were quite surprised but he had to have a drainage tube placed into the wound. I was forced to make a decision over letting one of them go, as it was simply not feasible to keep them in the same space. I couldn't stop Beau chasing the rabbit, nor could I keep T2 locked up. After making a few phone calls to see if anyone could help, I found a lady living in Emerald who was delighted to take on a male white, blue-eyed lop-eared rabbit.

It took Beau some adjusting as he continued to look for T2 in the garden. I found this upsetting to watch but could not possibly have kept on with the vet bills. I went on to acquire chickens thinking daily fresh eggs would be lovely, by which time they joined the nest, Beau had grown up a little. I had the rabbit hutches turned into a chicken coop and welcomed Pearl, a Barred Plymouth Rock, Hooter Bella, a Bantam Sussex and Francene, a striking Gold Laced Wyandotte. I also acquired the most handsome rooster I had ever seen who only lasted one night before he was re-homed to Chersterfield Farm. One very angry Corey and the neighbours complained they were being woken too early and would not accept a 4:30am wake-up alarm every morning. So I let him go.

I had a little chicken and she wouldn't lay an egg.
So I rubbed hot water up and down her leg.
The little chicken hollered; the little chicken begged.
But then the little chicken laid a hardboiled egg.

So now, I had my chickens, my aviary of Love Birds and beautiful Beau. Life was in a way, idyllic.
'*It's time to start a vegie patch,*' insisted Jon.
This life was blessed and prosperous.

♦

I remember going for many walks with Beau along the nearby bike track and Michael would often join us. We had many adventures and I cherished those *Magic Moments*. I would find myself carrying small logs or sticks home as though they were injured animals. Isobella loved these times with Michael too.

"Look, Nanny, there is a poor tiger," he would tell me and we would take it home to look after. Isobella truly believed that these were real animals and we tended to them with so much care and gentleness. They often became inhabitants of my garden. There were dogs with broken legs, horses with cuts and grazes, and other poorly injured creatures but the day Michael discovered the poor elephant I knew I was out of my depth, as he pointed towards what in reality was a huge tree stump.

"Let's just have a look at him, Michael, as I really don't think I can carry an elephant," I suggested.

So over we went, and as Michael looked at it, he picked up another piece of wood and rang a vet. "Hello, Doctor, we have found a poor elephant!" He put his hand over the make-believe speaker and said to me, "Nanny, the doctor says give it some water."

So Isobella held her scooped hands under the elephant's mouth and reported back to Michael, "It's okay, it is drinking now."

"Okay, thank you, Doctor", Michael said as he hung up on the vet. "He thinks it will be okay now, Nanny, but we should check on the way back."

Phew!

Another one of our walks turned out to be hysterical. It had been raining so Michael and I both had our wellington boots on. Beau also looked like he had his wellies on, for he liked walking in the wet grass or puddles which blackened his fair-coloured fur up to his knees. Then I came across a puddle which was a little larger than most and Isobella asked Michael if he could see the whale in it.

"Yes, I can," he said. "Shall we catch it?"

'Why not?' Isobella said, and we picked up some large sticks and proceeded to fish for the whale. I think Michael

got his fishing line caught on a snag, for as she watched him, he fell into the puddle. Up he emerged, wet right through and covered with mud.

Isobella was worried as he cried but all Poppet could do was giggle.

This turned into hysterical laughter for all Michael could say as he stumbled out was, "I want my mummy! I want my Nanny Thompson!"

Poor little bugger. We were having such a terrific time. I did check him over and even though he was cold and shivering there didn't seem to be any cuts or obvious broken bones, so we went back to the car.

Thankfully I had an old blanket in the car, so I stripped him out of his wet clothes and wrapped him up, leaving some for dirty Beau to sit on as well. The smell was rather putrid but I kept thinking, how would I get away with this? I know, we will go around the back and I can get him into the shower, but no! As soon as we were in the driveway, naked as a jay bird, he shot out of the car straight through the front door into his mother's arms.

All Jodie could say as she cuddled him (with a hint of sarcasm) was, "I can see you have been with your grandmother again."

"But it's not my fault," Isobella protested. "We were fishing for a whale when he just fell in!"

Poppet still found it hilarious and I caught Jodie looking at me.

Was there a hint of a smile?

♦

Over time it became glaringly obvious that I was no longer acknowledged as even being a part of my old family. I have many regrets about this and still hold slim hope that perhaps one day they will all apologise. It became incredibly awkward when family gatherings arose. I would attend but be forever on guard, watching closely over my shoulder in case my mother would approach. I knew she wanted the past left in the past, at all costs, and would often say, "It was so long ago, Denise, forget about it."

But I don't think she ever thought about how those actions impacted on me. It all still equated to a lifetime of struggle and her ignorance of this left me bewildered.

David remained in the background. I just couldn't bear him. Never an apology from him came my way, as though it was all my fault. His enduring presence was creepy and haunting. Things came to a head when Stacey, (my niece and Myra's daughter) hosted a party for her 21st birthday. Many guests attended and I could easily hide from Mum and David. I enjoyed mingling amongst the gathering.

It was a lovely night all round but when Mum and David quite suddenly made moves to leave, Mum was crying.

"Come on, David, we're going home," she sobbed.

Corey, who had had a few beers by this stage, walked with a slight sway towards me. "I am so sorry, Mum," he said out of nowhere.

"For what?" I asked.

"I just told your mum to fuck off."

"Why on Earth did you do that?" I asked.

"Well, she came up to me and asked how you were, so I told her to ask you herself. She said, 'We just don't understand and we don't know how to help her.' So I suggested she try and find out more about your condition, or just be there for you. She needs a mum and she can't understand why you're still with David."

He relayed back to me that Mum expressed she simply did not know what to do.

"Well, fuck off then!" was his response. "I'm so sorry, Mum," he reiterated.

The heated conversation took a while for me to wrap my head around. All the voices in my head were screaming, laughing, mortified, pointing out the funny side, but hell! I was worried about what might happen next. It was all too much for me to digest in the moment and as I looked around the party, I realised many of the guests had witnessed Mum's dramatic exit. Neither Myra nor Kerrie made any attempt to enquire what might have happened. My family did seem to have a history of having elephants in the room and this time was no different.

It dawned on me that night, though, that not only had my mother abandoned me but she had also abandoned Jodie and Corey. She was their grandmother, and they needed her too, but as usual, she neglected the heart of her familial responsibilities and went on maintaining her life with David. Perhaps it was all too much for her to accept about her partner, I do not know. What I do know now was that this estrangement I felt from her and my family at large, had a permanency about it, one that became cemented after my diagnoses. I made the decision to distance myself and focus on my health, my happiness, and a brighter future.

♦

No one seemed to notice, except Stacey, who one day asked me, "Aunty Niece, why don't you come down and visit the family anymore? It's not the same without you."

All I could say was that perhaps she should ask her mum. When Myra caught wind of the fact that Stacey was even in contact with me, she threatened me with a baseball bat if I were to tell her anything. But Stacey did persist! And I did eventually tell her the truth. I'm unsure of how things went down with the family thereafter.

On my Nana's 100th birthday I suffered extreme awkwardness at the occasion. I desperately wanted to attend and Jodie, Corey, Mark and Michael were attending also and promised to look out for me. Mum and David didn't say a word to us. Neither did my sisters. I remained infuriated with David for what he had done to me as a child and was also still angry with my mother. I had developed a knot of anxiety in the pit of my stomach, stewing over these unresolved feelings, which included feeling guilty for how I was feeling, as well as being judged by my family, to the point of estrangement.

'Go and do a letter drop to warn the neighbours about him,' coaxed Mizzy, who was certainly up for a bit of action. *'Or even paint a sign on his van.'*

'Let it go, my dear,' Spiritual One whispered. *'They are not worth it.'*

Plotting and scheming would get us nowhere, I decided, and only increased the turmoil and pain in my everyday world. My alters all wanted to help but the more we discussed it, the more my headaches compounded.

I discussed this ongoing predicament with Annabel, who informed me of a story about a woman who had been raped.

She went on to report it and when she was told how difficult the process would be, she pursued it anyway, wanting to at least have her day in court. When people asked her why, she said she wanted to claim her life back and make people see him for who he really was – a rapist. I resonated with her conviction and her story, and I wondered if I might find closure in the same way.

So I made an appointment with the Knox Police Sexual Assault team who listened to my case but informed me that if I charged him, he would most likely go to jail. I could not possibly have lived with the guilt of that outcome, so they suggested I take him to the Magistrates Court and charge him under Civil Law.

I was on a mission, a legal one this time. I was referred to a legal firm in the city and as there was no statute of limitations to sexual assault, they agreed to work with me and take up the challenge of my case. At the very least, I would have my day in court and that would be enough.

It was a lengthy process as I had to document so many reports – reports from Annabel, my doctor, the police and several psychiatrists. On the Friday prior to the Monday that I was due to appear in court, Jodie and I met with my legal advisors to ensure we were prepared for the court appearance. During that time, my solicitor took a phone call. It was from the Queen's Councillor (Galbally was the name mentioned) who was representing David. They advised that a loophole had been found in a recent clause that would make it impossible for me to win the case. For me to lose, would cost me all the legal fees and David's too. I was frightened and felt so vulnerable, so I just gave up.

Defeated and devastated at the time, I do look back on

this chapter and realise it was silly. I had no money, so how the hell would I pay for the case? I had just wanted my day in court so everyone could witness how awful David had been to me and that I had done nothing wrong but as it turned out, this was not to be a means for closure. This was not part of the plan.

♦

My therapy with Annabel became the focus and prioritising my mental health, a part of daily life now. There was a turning point after I had met with her for one of our sessions, whereby we seemed to cover a lot of ground and I got quite a load off my chest. The following day I woke up to a very strange experience.

I had woken up *before* my alters.

This had never happened. *Is this what's like to be normal?*

Rather than being dragged out of bed and plunged into the day with my guys all raring to go, madly clamouring around to get their day started, on this unusual morning, I woke up to peace.

Imagine, if you can, what it's like to be lying in bed still half asleep, when all of a sudden, the bedroom door opens and one of the kids notices you are awake. They in turn alert the others and they come rushing in, jumping on the bed, running around, poking and prodding you.

'Come on, get up!'

'Are we going to the beach today?'

'I want my breakfast.'

'Can we go out to play?'

'We've got to do the washing.'

'Maybe we could try and get organised?'
'Phone calls to make.'
'Have a shower.'
'Check your emails.'
'The animals need to be fed.'

And on and on it goes until you realise there will be no peace, no lying in bed, the day has already started. This is how it is for me and my *Unknown Friends Within*, as they set the tone for the day in such random and obtrusive ways. I drag myself out of bed, reach for a fag, flick the kettle on and try to gather *my* thoughts.

They are satisfied when I am up and about yet I am still half asleep. So I make coffee, switch on the computer and play a game or two of FreeCell to help align my focus. As I slowly regain consciousness my plans for the day ahead begin to unravel. Having been brutally woken up, I need a few minutes to find myself. What day is it? What time is it? And it all dawns on me as I delve into the computer games, that by focusing on the screen I am able to shut them off and come to terms with the breaking of a new day. I suppose it's a bit like Nana and her audio books. So as you can imagine, the morning I woke uninterrupted was very unreal and unnatural and yet, complete bliss!

Slight changes and advances in my world began to emerge, which I suppose were a result of all the work I was doing with Annabel. She helped me plough through the many ideas I had, and we discussed the various courses I was undertaking. It bothered me that I was dabbling in this and dabbling in that, taking snippets from a variety of workshops, then moving onto something else as quickly as I started. Was I a jill-of-all trades and master-of-none?

Annabel likened it to religion, which was another topic we'd been exploring. I had explained that I believed in reincarnation and a universal religion, as I could identify with the interconnected threads of them all. We also unpacked the notion of *blockages* – something that had come to my awareness as I delved deeper into healing modalities. For I had sat, engrossed in many lectures, be it for Care Ring, Shiatsu, Aromatherapy or Reiki and repeatedly heard of these things called *blockages*, defined as disharmonious blocks of energy that gather within the body that can cause physical ailments unless released.

My question for Annabel was, "Whose blockages are they?" For each of my alters had their own emotional baggage, or perhaps they were blockages, yet we all shared the same body. We are like a jigsaw within the jigsaw that is me.

For example, Poppet's blockages are isolated to my stomach where I experience intolerable knots of pain. I know she has held that pain for years, so no wonder I now suffer Diverticulitis Disease, Irritable Bowel Syndrome and pain associated with breaking wind. Is it any wonder I have endured such long episodes of depression? The stresses each one of my alters has been through were never properly dealt with, addressed or resolved. Therefore, I would think it was natural that the chemical imbalances and hormonal changes present in my physiology manifested as symptoms of depression.

These were the topics of conversation I delved into with Annabel, and I developed a keen interest in learning to heal myself. Whether that be using Reiki, aromatherapy or meditation, I was on a new mission to bring my body into harmony again; to release my blockages and that of my alters. My journal writing was also very significant as I had kept up a solid writing practise over the years, documenting my experiencing and using writing as a tool for contemplation, catharsis and storytelling.

"Have you shown it to anyone yet?" I asked Annabel. I didn't have a problem about her doing so and she said it would not have been ethical. I gave her my permission and have meanwhile held onto an inner knowing that one day my journaling would assist the development of my own book devoted to my experience of DID.

Writing, specifically stream of consciousness writing, has helped me clarify so many scattered bits and pieces that had I not externalised my thoughts through writing them out, I would have gone completely round the twist, even further!

'Like you're not now?' teased Mizzy.

'Thank you, Mizzy.'

◆

Spending time with my grandchildren continued to be a source of joy. Christopher, my second grandchild and brother to Michael was in day care when the 2008 Olympic games were held and one morning, one of the day care staff was laminating small cards with all the competing country's flags on them. There were 84 in total and to keep Christopher entertained, she suggested that as she finished each card, that he might like to try and remember them. By the end of the day, much to her amazement, Christopher was able to identify all 84 flags. She allowed Jodie to bring them home so that we could see how clever he was. Sure enough, he could pick each and every one of them. Some of the countries I hadn't even heard of, but I did love to hear his pronunciation of *Bots-wainia.*

Christopher told his Uncle Corey that there were some kids who were meant for walking (I think he was referring to Michael) and some that weren't. "I think, Uncle Corey, I am one of those."

When spending time with Michael I was able to return to being a little girl during our nature walks but with Christopher, a game of chess or cards played by his rules was my inroad back to my inner child. He and I had a few childish spats and thoroughly enjoyed ourselves.

Then came the day he introduced me to a computer game called *Wizard 101.* Poppet was intrigued and she would watch him closely then ask if she could have a go.

He suggested that I go home, download the game and come up with an avatar for myself so we could play together online. He would show me what to do and how to play once I had done that. Poppet couldn't wait, so as soon as I had finished my dinner, I was on the computer downloading *Wizard 101* and creating our avatar.

I rang the next day and asked Christopher if it was okay for me to come over that night and start playing.

"Hang on, Nanny," he said, as he yelled out to his mum to ask permission.

"Only if you get your homework done first," I heard Jodie reply.

"She said yes, Nanny, and I will ring you when I have finished my homework."

After finishing his homework, he did ring and off I went.

We loaded up *Wizard 101* and I showed him my avatar.

"Oh my goodness, you have to be kidding me, Nanny!' and he promptly set to work on her, changing its clothes and changing its hair. I found myself wondering why I had bothered but it was all in good fun and we a great time.

When it was time for Christopher to start getting ready for bed, I felt a bit lost. I had to remember he was off to school the next day and needed his sleep. But where did that leave me? I had to switch again but I did promise Poppet there would be many more play times in the future. And that is how my first play date with my grandson ended.

Christopher and I shared many games with each other, but he stunned me when he looked straight at me one day and said, "Nanny, I really think you need to get out there a bit more. Have you ever thought about joining *eHarmony*?"

"Goodness gracious no, I haven't Christopher."

"Well you should, Nanny. I'll do the application for you. What have you got to lose?"

After the work he had done on my avatar for *Wizard 101*, I thought maybe my pride would be my first guess, for heaven knows what he thought my profile should look like.

"Go on, Nanny," he said.

"Thank you very much, darling, but no, I will give it a miss thank you."

"Well, just keep it in mind. I will help you if you change your mind."

I really didn't know whether to laugh or feel humbled by this offer but it did make me wonder if I needed to get out more.

♦

An example of how I have minimised events and have done so all my life, which is typically a feature of my condition, was highlighted back in 2011 when I was having problems with my glasses. I thought I had sat on them or something, as everything seemed out of focus. I took myself to Specsavers to get them adjusted.

It seemed my glasses were fine but the optometrist said he wanted to check my eyes. He seemed concerned and referred me on for a second opinion. I asked Jodie to drive me to the new appointment and didn't really know what to expect.

On the day of the appointment, I was given various dyes and drops put in my eyes and after a number of scans, I was called in to see the doctor. He asked Jodie to come in as well as he felt I may need support. I hadn't really been overly concerned, until now.

"I am sorry to say but you have Wet Macular Degeneration in your left eye," the doctor announced.

"Oh! So what happens now?" I asked.

"We cannot cure it but we can manage it with injections."

It didn't seem to be a big deal so I asked him when I could start. He realised that I didn't really understand what he had said, so went on to explain that the injection would be given directly in my eye on a monthly basis. Jodie nearly fell off her chair and I just sort of went numb.

'Pull yourself together girl,' Logical One said. *'What other option do you have, go blind?'*

The doctor then went on to say that I could have the injection there and then, or I could go away and think about it.

'God! Who wants to think about?' said Mizzy. *'Just say yes and*

it will be all over soon.'

'But what about next time?' cried Poppet.

'Don't think about that right now, let's just get this one out of the way.'

I knew that Logical One was right.

So with the help of my team, I felt ready to go ahead. Poor Jodie, I don't know how she was feeling about it as it was all happening so quickly. I went to the surgery room on the lower floor and was ushered into the pre-op room where a lovely nurse reassured me that it wasn't as bad as all that. She would be putting some numbing drops in my eye before the doctor would administer the injection.

Several drops later and the doctor standing behind me saying, "Look up" and it was all done and dusted – no big deal! This is how I tend to step aside and let the others take over. Since then my right eye had developed WMD and also needed to be injected but I must admit, it really is not as bad as it sounds.

I was having ongoing problems with my right eye though. It wasn't responding to the treatment as well as my left and I bought this up with the doctor by saying, "Isn't it funny how you can have two eyes that react so differently?"

To which he replied quite seriously, "Well, they don't know about each other."

"Oh, is that why we have our nose in the middle of our face? So, they can't see each other!" asked Poppet. A sensible question, one would think but the doctor thought it was hilarious.

"Well, I haven't heard that before," he chuckled.

How childish I must have sounded but it was a question from Poppet, after all.

148

♦

Due to my mental health, I have not been able to work in the same capacity as I once had, so I started to look for alternative means of income, enough to keep my head above water. I had thrown in the towel with dog and rabbit breeding as it pulled too heavily at my heart strings, and my interest in health and wellbeing had led me to studying meditation and relaxation massage. I enrolled in a course to become a Meditation Teacher and took up complimentary study in Reiki.

I kind of bluffed my way through the initial business stages, setting up space from home to offer massage in the spare bedroom and meditation training in the lounge area. All my alters jumped on board when it came to decorating the space and trying to decide upon fabric for cushions was a jolly nightmare. I recall walking out of one of the shops saying out loud, "That's enough! We are not buying any cushions today. I cannot take it anymore. We are going to get my hair cut." When lo and behold I had turned into that woman, the one that Corey feared I would become.

One of my first customers ended up propositioning me, which put another spanner in the works and was the last thing I needed in my new burgeoning career. It was my first client and my meditation teacher had referred him onto me but something didn't feel right from the get-go. When I arrived at my teacher's rooms, I was introduced to a gentleman who smiled and thanked me for coming. We were ushered to a room for the massage to take place and my teacher then left us alone. I asked him to make himself feel comfortable and to call out to me once he was undressed and lying face down on the table. This was when I began to realise just how gullible and naïve I can be.

"No, you stay," he insisted. "I want you to take your clothes off now!"

I explained that I wasn't doing *that* sort of massage and promptly left the rooms. I never did return and felt rather silly. Nor did I ever attend a meditation class there again.

My solution was to set-up a massage table in a ladies' hairdressing salon in a space where the waxing usually took place. I felt more comfortable being in the company of others and began averaging about two or three massages a day. Both men and women booked in for sessions and they were genuinely lovely clients but on one day, one exceedingly awful day, I decided to call it quits. It was due to a man who visited and asked about my prices, but more specifically, "How much for a happy ending?"

With my massage and meditation plans now gone out the window, I still had a firm commitment in my heart to tend to my own healing and recovery journey. I pursued further study in Reiki, and Carmel joined me on an immersive retreat. It was a weekend of adventure and pleasurable time spent together. I returned, a qualified Reiki masseur, even though the entire course remains much of a blur.

♦

As time went on, I felt that I could take on more volunteer work as it became clear that I would probably never return to a mainstream work environment. I did, however, see the value in being part of a team, contributing in the workplace and having a purpose in terms of role and responsibilities.

I did the ring-around to offer my services to a few organisations, but it was the Mental Illness Fellowship (MIF) who called me, that set me on my path to becoming a valued member of the organisation.

They were looking for volunteers to sell raffle tickets. I thought, *Why the hell not? I have a mental illness*, and so I went about selling tickets for almost three years, by which time I had ran out of people to ask to buy the tickets. I felt guilty about letting them know that I simply could not go on in my pursuit of ticket sales, when it dawned on me, one cold morning as I was warming my backside up against the wall heater, that surely I could volunteer my services in a better way.

I decided to call them and explain that I had a mental illness and would I be able to help the organisation in any way. The lived experience story was gaining more recognition in the mental health sector during this time. It was an exciting wave of change as our voices were becoming heard, respected and drawn on to inform how mental health services operated. But I was not so aware of this on a broader scale; I was at the beginning of my own journey of recovery and instinctively knew I had something to offer.

"Hello, Brendon speaking," said a man's voice down the phone. The conversation that followed was the beginning of a wonderful friendship.

Brendon asked me many questions and I provided him with honest answers. I was totally transparent about my condition and felt naturally at ease discussing it with him.

"How do you feel about public speaking?" he asked.

I told him I had previously spoken publicly about DID and that I enjoyed it, and so it became that I was invited to join a new group called the Speakers Bureau and receive training in public speaking. The aim of the group was to shed light on what it was like living with a mental illness and that through the power of storytelling, misconceptions about mental illness could be demystified and the thick stigma that surrounded people with an experience of mental illness could be challenged.

I felt so comfortable in the group and had a natural affinity with the role of being a Peer Support Worker, who was someone with a mental illness who could be of support to another person having their own experience of mental illness. Even though my involvement with MIF was all new to me, I found it very exciting and meaningful to be a part of. Brendon, who also had an experience of mental illness, was an inspiring role model for me.

His confidence and commitment to the role was infectious and I learned a lot through working by his side. I felt I had come home in this workplace environment of peers who had common ground in the stories we shared about our tumultuous lives and personal struggles, yet we were strongly bound by our shared humanity, our strength and empathy. On the day of the first training when Brendon introduced himself, I recall saying to myself, *I want to be a Brendon!* And I knew in my heart that I could.

I went on to centre stage, doing many presentations in schools, universities and communities. The dissolution of stigma was almost palpable as I sensed audience members recognising more of the truth about people's struggles with mental illness rather than the inaccurate portrayals and ideas they had in their minds, caused very much so by the media and a lack of understanding within society in general.

Stigma in the community was one element we were tackling. There was self-stigmatisation too.

Poppet and I had come to terms with having developed very low-self-esteem over the years of having a mental illness and the idea that we had failed in life was a strong belief I worked steadily at breaking down. My role at MIF helped me to do so.

When I had previously decided to do a Certificate IV in Training and Assessment, I recall feeling very much out of my depth in a group full of nurses, teachers and students who were all much younger than me. I had hoped to bluff my way through the training, as I had done so on many occasions throughout my life but this time proved different. I could not understand what the tutor was talking about nor keep up with the work required of me. I ended up dropping out after three lectures and was confronted by the fact that my mental illness was contributing to my lack of capabilities.

When the faculty head called me the next term to see if I might be continuing, I had already decided that I could not return as I was not cut out with the right skills. I was convinced my DID had impacted my abilities. When I explained this over the phone, the organiser said that none of the participants were able to follow the training and that the lecturer had been dismissed. There would be a new tutor on board next term if I wanted to return.

And so I did. I returned and completed the training after all, with the lesson learned that perhaps I should not be so hard on myself for having a mental illness and that I was as capable of doing anything I set out to achieve with a little effort and perseverance.

I gained my Certificate IV in Training and Assessment

and chose beekeeping as my subject – an area I was just as passionate about it as Jon and Isobella and already had much knowledge due to keeping my own bees.

'*Mmmm, you always have to be different don't you. They didn't even know you could do a course in bee keeping*,' Logical One pointed out with a smile.

"Of course I could. It was part of the Department of Primary Industries, and I was a registered bee keeper."

♦

My first Lived Experience Presentation was an exciting, pivotal moment. I was supported on the day by a more experienced presenter; but unfortunately, I don't remember many details of the event. The feedback I got from the audience, Brendon and my fellow presenter, Larry, was overwhelmingly positive.

"They loved it!" said Larry to Brendon. "Especially when she talked about <such-and-such>."

Perhaps it was a good thing that I could not recall what I shared, and I wondered which of my alters had taken over to tell our tales. I knew some of them enjoyed the limelight too and could only hope they had behaved themselves.

The presentation I remember most fondly was at a private Melbourne boy's college as it involved what I call, a *Magic Moment.* As I left the archaic, imposing building feeling uplifted after a successful presentation, I paused, transfixed by the sight of a storm rolling in from the west. The city had disappeared under dark clouds that enveloped everything in their wake. Everyone was rushing towards their car. Wild wind swept up leaves, rubbish and dust, churning and whirling it every-which-way with enormous energy. It was exhilarating to watch, and I was transfixed.

The weather had turned on a dime and I stood still amongst the chaos. Darkness and noise fell upon me and lamps switched on, as if on cue. I was in a captivating fantasy and the imposing building reminded me of Hogwarts – land of awe and wonder. Eerie were my surrounds and the associated sounds of the storm. Poppy and Mizzy were also transfixed as the rain began pouring heavily upon us. It brought me back to the present moment and I had to hurry along to find my car. Boy did we get a soaking! But regardless of being drenched to my socks, I felt alive, happy and liberated. It was definitely a *Magic Moment.*

'Get home and dry yourself off. You will catch a shocking cold, girl!' insisted Marm.

'We can be so adventurous, can't we?' I don't know if Mizzy was taking the mickey or if she too was overwhelmed by the sheer brilliance of Mother Nature. It was but a few days after this memorable moment that I received an email from Brendon, forwarding some feedback on from my presentation. It read:

Hey guys,

Some quick communication regarding Xavier College. Firstly, I must say that I really enjoyed presenting to this college. The boys, I felt, got a great deal from it and particularly on conclusion of the first presentation, more than half the boys made their business to shake my hand and thank me. All teachers involved were very thankful.

I got to meet Peter Duckworth (the senior coordinator of the senior campus) this morning who had already had some feedback from the previous day that was very glowing. He also let me know

that his boy was in Denise's group and that his boy couldn't stop talking about the presentation all night ... Peter was over the moon.
Cheers,
Stephen

'We done well!' said Poppet.
Mmmm, nice to hear, I thought. *'Indeed Poppet, we, done well.'*

I have since received a lot of positive feedback and it makes me realise how talking openly about mental health issues is so important. I am very determined and committed to 'fly the flag'. In my own way with my unique story, I know I am breaking down stigma in small but impactful ways. The art of storytelling is a very powerful tool indeed.

I have now spent many years being part of the MIF Speaker's Bureau Team. I have given presentations on my Lived Experience to a variety of high school students, psychologists, counsellors and members of community centres. I have travelled interstate to participate in public speaking events and have immensely loved the adventure it has taken me on. I have developed a strong sense of self-worth, something I have never felt before in my life and I am endlessly grateful to MIF – now called Wellways – for granting me with the opportunity to serve the community and be supported on my own journey of self-empowerment too.

My role as a speaker evolved to co-facilitation with Brendon in the future training of new recruits and as I went from strength-to-strength in the Peer Support environment I witnessed many others do the same. I found the facilitation in this space to be the most rewarding, as it was a safe place for our true-life stories to be heard, witnessed and subsequently, healed. So much about mental health issues are shrouded in silence, so the opportunity to set our stories free is incredibly liberating.

I continued to train facilitators and also facilitated programs myself. The Recovery Program was offered to groups of 8–10 people in a three-hour session, once a week, over the course of 10 weeks. These programs were facilitated by Peer Support workers with the aim of helping others identity the causes and effects of their symptoms. Once awareness was drawn to these symptoms, they could build a toolbox to help manage them in daily life.

Even though I facilitated these programs, I always regarded myself as a participant too, learning new tools and techniques to manage my condition and enact self-care. It was rich and diverse hearing everybody's different viewpoints and the experiences they were having.

Another service that became available through Wellways was the 'Understanding Mental Illness' program which both Brendon and I were in the thick of facilitating, sharing the Lived Experience component of each program. These were educational presentations for different public sectors, which identified and explained what it was like to experience mental health issues. Many workplaces and community centres took advantage of these sessions and I felt very proud and passionate to be a part of them.

The following email highlights the impact we achieved:

Dear Tim,

This morning I attended one of your Understanding Mental Illness workshops put on by the Boroondara volunteer resource centre. It was conducted by Brendon and Denise, and I would just like to say what an outstanding job they did. It was an excellent morning, and I can't thank them enough for their generosity in sharing their experiences and knowledge with us.

Their frankness in discussing their own lives was inspiring and I don't think there could be a better way of helping the community to becoming more open, aware, and accepting of mental illness than attending their session.

I will certainly use the workshop to initiate discussion with my family and friends. For anyone working in or wanting to work in the mental health area the workshop would be invaluable. From my own personal point of view as someone with a family member who has a mental illness, it has been enormously helpful and given me hope.

So again, a big thank you with best wishes,
Ann.

I sent a copy of this to Corey and his reply was just as heart-warming to me.

Hi Mum,
I don't know if I replied to this, but this is fantastic. This is the sort of feedback that so many people don't get so for you to influence someone enough for them to take time out of their own day to email, is good.

Congrats and well done.

I enjoyed the work I was doing and my friendship with Brendon grew very meaningful to me. We continue to this day to be the best of pals. Brendon, myself and my alters have shared many experiences through co-facilitating as well as simply through sharing strong friendship. He is a brilliant mentor in my life.

My guys were ever-present and he handled them gracefully. If he thought they were overriding with too much switching and input during presentations, he would suggest I get a glass of water or take a break and would pick up where I left off. Mizzy could be outrageous sometimes, driving poor Brendon to almost lose the plot but we would always end up having a good laugh.

And there were elements of magic shining through my training days. I recall one morning as I travelled on the train to Richmond, I looked around and saw that everyone was on their devices. I was simply sitting, wondering how the day might pan out but as the train pulled into Blackburn station, I glanced out and saw a possum slowly climbing down the rock walkway.

The train came to a standstill. I stopped, the possum stopped, and I swear to god, our eyes locked ever so briefly. As the train resumed its ride my friend, the possum, continued on his climb. As I looked back around the carriage, no one had experienced that *Magic Moment*, only myself and Isobella who was smiling. I too smiled (on the inside) and I felt sorry for all and sundry. I felt so blessed to share that *Magic Moment* with such a lovely creature.

♦

I have since wondered by helping all these other people through my volunteer work, that perhaps my alters are the ones who have been ignored all this time, and that's why my head continues to hurt. When I am tired, they make so much noise, all trying to win my attention and tell me the things they would like to do – it's difficult to satisfy them all. Someone once commented on how I am always so active and busy.

If only they understood that I am not the only one who is busy, there are my alters who have lives of their own too. I have so many projects on the go, with everything due to be finished yesterday!

When the National Disability Insurance Scheme was slowly being rolled out across Australia, I felt it was somewhat unfortunate for me and my peer workers, for previously we were working for a not-for-profit organisation and the government would fund our Community and Peer Education Schemes.

I personally feel that the NDIS is more focussed on physically disabled people, which is a positive outcome; however, it is now up to the individuals with mental health issues to seek and pay for services out of their NDIS packages. So even though I am still a mental health advocate and working to break down stigma within communities, it is not quite the same as when I took up the role. I do not get paid for my work but whenever anyone approaches me, I will, as a peer, try to help. It is my hope that someday mental health issues will be addressed more directly again.

'Who knows what lies around the next bend, pet?' reminded Spiritual One.

Nothing stays the same forever, I always say, and I occasionally grow hyper-excited about what the future may hold. For even though I may be going through a rough time, I know deep inside now that I will always bounce back.

'You always do, and it is a credit to you that you are sometimes

able to see the funny side of things that others can't,' said Logical One.

'Ever the optimist, that's you and don't ever minimise your sense of humour.'

Having said all that, as my time with Wellways has slowly dwindled off, I have had more time to concentrate on completing this book now and want to take the opportunity to share some final words about myself and my journey with my *Unknown Friends Within.*

PART FOUR

The Present Day

I now live in a community housing unit and even though some of my alters are not happy about it, I never thought I'd end up here either; I understand their grievances. My grandson, Christopher, once said to me while we were taking Beau for a walk, "Beau seems to be so happy here as there are many places he can run and play."

"Yes," I agreed. "What about me though?"

"Why Nana, what's wrong with it?"

"It just seems to be so small," I said.

"Well how much room does one person need?" He was right and I wondered when he had become so wise.

I have a roof over my head, food on the table every day and I repeatedly find myself saying, "Nothing stays the same forever". I can't ever help wondering what lies around the next corner.

In 2014 my granddaughter was born, Imogen Daisy Young. When she is asked her name, she makes a point of proudly saying, Imogen Daisy Young. She was actually my third grandchild and daughter to Corey and Susie. Imogen could be described as quite feminine by comparison to the other females in the family, stubbornly refusing to wear jeans or track suits and favouring her tulle dancing skirts matched with stockings. She now takes dancing and singing lessons. This quality in her stands out for me as she represents the little girl I was never allowed to be.

'And what's wrong with that?' Mizzy asked.

'I would have been too scared to do that,' said Poppet.

I am so proud of her and her authentic self-expression, and I love her dearly. Watching her dance and sing on stage brings me so much joy; however, I don't get to see her often as they live on the other side of the city. I usually stay over the weekend for the travelling doesn't leave me much time with her if I did it in one day. She has her swimming lessons on Sunday mornings, and I do get to see her in the pool. After her lessons, I have spent time with her in the water and that is good too.

She is forever playing with her dolls, which all have names seemingly borrowed from story books and cartoon characters. She lives in a world of princes and princesses, and I enjoy sitting with her for hours on end, usually getting all the names mixed up as we play. Together we share a world of make-believe and I encourage her imagination to soar. I know now from experience that a little bit of imagination can go a long way in life and Imogen reflects back to me all that is innocent and playful about childhood.

Like the day I was supposed to be the driver of the bus (the lounge room settee) and all of them were piled in, and we were going to Altona.

"All aboard, sit down and off we go," we announce in our make-believe worlds.

Then one of them would need to go to the toilet.

"I did ask you all if you had been before we headed off," Jon says as the gruff bus driver pulling over to let one of them off at the stop.

Imogen would giggle as this was not the only stop we would ever make along the way. I was truly in a world of make-believe again and a trip that should have only taken 15 minutes becomes an ongoing saga. Many stops with the gruff bus driver threatening to take them all home if they didn't behave!

I managed to catch Susie and Corey spying on us once, having a bit of a laugh. Did I care? No. Jon loved being the gruff bus driver, and Isobella and Poppet were among the princes and princess, I believe it was them who stirred the other passengers on.

So life on the whole is now much calmer and filled with these precious moments of time spent with the people I love. I continue to focus on my health and still require a network of practitioners to keep an eye on all facets of my wellbeing. I have tried many different GPs over the years, and was even once refused by one who admitted he didn't know much about DID. I appreciated his honesty (and luckily wasn't charged for the consultation).

I now have a great GP called Melanie. I feel she understands me and my idiosyncrasies. I can talk openly and honestly with Melanie and always feel comfortable after a visit. She has guided me to see a number of psychologists and psychiatrists and been very patient with me when I have found some of her suggestions unsuitable. My support team has changed over the years, but I now have Melanie, a psychologist called Christina, and a psychiatrist, Dr Kalra, who is very interested in learning more about my condition.

There is an additional alter whom I have not yet mentioned in this book, who I would like to introduce now. His name is Bob and, in my eyes, he's a bit of a hero. Bob held himself back for many years but I now know he has always been with me. My fascination with Bob is based on the fact that on many occasions when I have been engaging in discussions with people, if there has been any hint of an argument arising, Bob would come to the fore. He would take on any challenge in calm and clever ways, which definitely does not come naturally to me.

Bob, I now realise, was the one who loved Physics, Chemistry and Maths back at secondary school. He always encouraged me to question the many wonders of the universe, particularly anything to do with metaphysics; the branch of philosophy that examines the fundamental nature of reality. We have both always been fascinated with the relationship between mind and matter, substance and attribute, and potentiality and actuality. The wonders of the world never cease to amaze me, and I/we have also been drawn to studying the microphysical, the branch of physics that deals with bodies and phenomena on a microscopic/ smaller scale, especially with molecules, atoms and subatomic particles to the far reaches of the universe and everything else in between. The wonders of the world never cease to amaze me.

So whenever Professor Brian Cox, who is an astrophysicist and Professor of Particle Physics is mentioned, Bob and I are in our element.

I do find it incredible how I am inhabited by so many personalities. They are, on the one hand, very different with their own thoughts and opinions, yet on the other, share commonalities of interest. For example, the unlikely match of Spiritual One and Bob. They share passionately over science and metaphysics as well as spirituality, but at the end of the day have respect for each other's varying opinions. They are the yin and yang, you could say. I find it quite the struggle sometimes to find a happy balance between all of them, so that we can reside together in harmony. It is forever a work-in-progress.

I can illustrate this better through example. Even in the most mundane scenarios, I have competing thoughts and opinions of my alters racing through me. One evening, as I was retiring for sleep, I looked over at my bedroom chair. It had a pair of slacks draped across it as well as my teddy bear heat pack. Now the way my slacks have fallen has caught Isobella's attention. The teddy bear's nose and one big brown eye is peeking from underneath. I decide to cover teddy, for I can't help but keep glancing at him with his one eye staring back at me.

'For goodness sake,' says Logical One. *'He is only a stuffed heat pack. He is not real.'*

'Yes he is. He is very real!' insists Isobella.

And as I look around the room, I see many stuffed animals. A yellow duck, two puppies, a floppy dog. To Logical One, toys are all that they are – stuffed animals – but to Isobella, they are very real. They are her friends, and she loves them.

This seems a minor detail to write about but it highlights what can engage me throughout the day, as my mind and my friends within ponder everything, and often with mixed opinions and desires. Even a subtle move, such as keeping the toys in a dark room could upset Isobella and send her into spin, but of course Logical One, Mizzy and Spiritual One, are likely to chime in too. I guess what I am trying to say is that simple things are not so straight-forward for me and this is what it is like, day-to-day, living and breathing DID.

'Thank you for letting me keep my friends,' says Isobella. *'I know that they wouldn't like it in the dark but I don't know what you mean about me being in the dark. I am not in the dark. It would be nasty in the dark but they are real, and they love me and I love them. They are so cute and I don't want them to be frightened. My daddy is in the dark, in a big hole in the dark and that's not nice to think about, so I won't.'*

Now a question from Poppet. *'Why didn't Mummy marry Maurice? I liked him. He was Daddy's friend and he loved us. I can remember Daddy, Maurice and Mummy before the darkness came, singing and playing records. Dean Martin mostly, and Nat King Cole. And I remember another friend of my daddy's – Mark someone. He ended up in a mental institution and we would visit him. I don't know why he was there. Mummy explained he was tired but I remember him singing* Til I Kissed You *by the Everly Brothers, and every time I hear that song, I think about him. I feel both happy and sad.'*

I don't really care what other people may think of me – this is all very normal to us. When I'm watching TV, Isobella and I break out in conversation and because all our toy animals have personalities and are very much alive to us, they seem to understand what we are saying. If we walk into a shop together and there are soft, cuddly toys, we love to pick them up and have a cuddle and a chat.

We both find it heartbreaking to put them down and leave them. I guess you could say this is all relative to still keeping a connection with my inner-child alive, despite all the trauma and haunting memories associated with it. I have Isobella to thank for this, and also to ensure she gets to connect with whatever makes her happy, be it acquiring more animals or toys in our home.

Music is another area that distinctively conveys my different personalities. I have always loved music and when I reflect on my early childhood, I still recall fondly the classic hits of Dean Martin, Nat King Col, The Platters, Harry Belafonte and so many others of that era. As I have developed numerous alters, so has the variety of genres I like expanded. Each of my personalities have their favourites, from Irish Ballads, Elvis, Classical, Il Divo and the Tenors, Queen and Freddy Mercury, John Williamson and English balladeers such as Ed Sheeran and James Blunt. I feel an emotive connection with them all and my iTunes playlists is indicative of the many styles of music me and my alters like to listen to.

Music and the anecdotal evidence of my 'childish' love of animals and stuffed toys are simple examples of the full spectrum of differences I have learned to live with in order to keep all of my alters happy. I can't stress enough what a push-pull scenario takes shape in my mind every day and how exhausting this is for me to attempt to even manage. It seems impossible to please all my alters and yet I get caught up in a struggle of trying to do so.

Meeting the needs of 12 different characters is thoroughly

challenging and, in a way, the story of my life. I yearn to lead a more 'normal' existence; to just get up, take a shower, make the bed, have some breakfast – to step into the day with ease and flow. I do not know what I would do without Logical One who at least offers guidance that sets much of the chaos straight, no matter how short-term her advice is.

'Get organised, my dear,' she says, *'So that once you have the morning chores done, then the day is yours. You can maybe even tick a couple of tasks off The Lists.'*

Did I do any chores this morning? Oh no, of course not! I have been sitting here writing instead of doing all the things that are yet to be done. Bugger! I haven't even finished yesterday's jobs.

There are slacks all over the lounge floor, the remnants of my wardrobe strewn everywhere from beginning to sort through my clothes but not finishing the job. A basket of damp washing has not yet been hung out to dry and will need to be rinsed now, before hanging. I wander about the house, unable to focus properly but noticing an empty bottle here, a misplaced cushion there.

'Throw everything on the floor and start tomorrow,' suggests Mizzy.

Dishes are everywhere and a lot of honey buckets all over the floor, waiting to be washed and re-used. Unopened mail is scattered on my bed and there's shopping that still needs to be put away. There is stuff everywhere. Filing, book papers, CDs to be burnt and bank statements to be sorted.

My bed linen hasn't been changed for weeks and even though I've attempted to strip it, it still hasn't made it to a wash. I can sleep on the couch. There are too many clothes and blankets and a half-emptied suitcase tossed on it anyhow. I take a moment to stand still amongst the chaos to ponder my dilemma, totally overwhelmed as to where to start and when it all might end, with my head beginning to throb at the thought of it.

All the rooms in my life seem to be in turmoil. The best analogy I can find is that of throwing a party and waking up the next day to face the results of a debaucherous night. Not one room has been left untouched and I query how I will find the energy to get things back in order, if ever there was a semblance of order. I like the motivation, yet I am consistently tired. I'd prefer to take my medication and head to bed.

I remain lost in a cacophony of voices and have trouble remembering whether I have washed my hair or not, so I give it another wash, just in case. The only way I can gain some control is by saying, *'I am now washing my hair,'* as though I have to claim my actions and behaviour then follow through to keep my alters at bay. It's the only way I know how to master the moment. I say, "I am now doing the dishes", or "I am changing the sheets", and they just must accept that this is what is happening. It is much like a chant and a meditation. I suppose it keeps me anchored in the present moment. It definitely helps to stop the torrent of voices interrupting me with every move I make.

Ultimately, though, it is this book that is causing everyone so much anxiety.

'Why?' asks Logical One.

'Cos, silly,' says Poppet. *'What if no one likes it?'*

'Let alone, understands it,' remarks Mizzy with her classic jocularity.

I, too, am feeling very anxious and my doubts are many

and varied. I am curious if this is the normal response to divulging my life's story through a book or whether my mental health condition is exacerbating my insecurities. Despite the overwhelming feelings, a very real passion burns within me, convincing me that my story has merit and will benefit others struggling with mental health issues.

It's the lingering shadow of stigma that hovers over my pages and the 'labels' we've acquired that create misunderstandings about the truth. Of who we are, of how we got here, where we came from and where we are going. So unfair and unnecessary is the grip of mental health misconception.

♦

To conclude, to say I have had a colourful life is a bit of an understatement but closest to the truth. I have had many different jobs, lived in over 12 different houses and consider myself a 'Jill-of-all-Trades, Master-of-None'. And still, I have not yet mentioned all my work and life experiences in this book.

'*No, we really don't have enough time for all of them to be mentioned. Maybe another time,*' suggests Poppet.

I can't say if this journey of change and moving about is over yet, who knows?

'*Well God does, doesn't he, pet?*' says Spiritual One. I try to cut her off for I don't really want to call in another venture, yet there is truth in her words. There is The Plan!

She continues regardless. '*The future is clouded for good reason. You are not meant to know what lies beyond the next corner. Anything is possible and nothing is impossible. There will always be something. As your awareness expands, so do the possibilities.'*

I continue to sleep a lot. Fatigue is a permanent state of being. I say my prayers out loud and then curse, just as loudly. Then suddenly find myself digging and turning the compost or re-potting another of my favourite plants when really, I should be hanging out the washing or making the bed.

I'm not so sure I have fully comprehended how differently I see, hear, and feel things compared to other people but there is not much I can do about that, I suppose.

You may find me wandering aimlessly around my unit trying to decide what to do next but unable to concentrate on any one, particular task. So I pace between rooms until finally asking myself, *Now what the hell was it I was going to do?*

My mind is rarely still. I'm always thinking but never about a single thing.

'Quickly write that down,' Logical One says.

'No, the dishes need to be done,' butts in Marm.

'Well, do the dishes and just add it to The List,' says Logical One.

Boy, do I have lists! They are all over the place and consistently need to be gathered up and reconciled.

'Well, put that in the diary under Jobs to be Done – Sort out lists!' says Mizzy.

But where on Earth is my diary?

You might find me sitting in a corner crying my eyes out. Know that something has clearly upset me! But if you were to look away for a moment, in the blink of an eye, I have changed. I am laughing my head off at the thought of a funny joke. Or had I? Perhaps it was one of my alters...

Then again, I may just be sitting, staring into nothingness. I am not there, I am nowhere, but I am still here.

Why does this all happen? Who knows.

It's just how it is and will always be, for me, for them and for *us*.

SIMONE'S INTERVIEW

She is dressed for the weather in a comfortable tracksuit and slippers, it is frosty outside, and the wall heater brings warmth to the living room. She walks gently, controlled through the dining room to the kitchen to prepare a pot of tea. She stops briefly on the way by the glass doors framing the aviary of love birds on the far side of the backyard.

Sliding the door open just enough to welcome her best friend, Beau, a fluffy white dog bounds in and dances around her feet. Forced to step backwards a pool of sunlight captures the warmth in her eyes as she smiles adoringly.

Those eyes are a window into the world where Denise lives with her 12 other selves. Denise has Dissociative Identity Disorder (DID) formerly known as multiple personalities.

Taking her tea and settling on the floral sofa in the living room, Denise slides off her slippers and curls her legs up on the sofa beside her. Beau lays faithfully at the tip of her toes.

Her suburban living room could belong to any 57-year-old mother. Like the rest of the house, it is clean and tidy, photos of an adult son and daughter share wall space with treasured grandchildren.

On the table lay a small clue that something is different, a pile of lists and reminders, for Denise a necessary part of everyday life. On the floor a large bag cradles a lifetime of memories on pages soon to become the memoirs of a complicated existence.

In a well-educated Australian accent Denise speaks fondly of her childhood prior to her father's sudden death and the onset of DID. The family lived in a large house on Beach

Road, Mentone, now a highly sort after beach side area of Melbourne. She describes them as the average happy family.

As the eldest of three sisters, she felt particularly close to her father, her face softens warmly as she vividly recounts a shoulder ride at the age six then dulls through the rehashing of his sudden death just four years after. The trauma proved too great for her young mind and for six months she retreated into a catatonic state of which she has no recollection. Rigorously reminded 'she is the big girl' Denise feels an enormous burden to take care of her mother and two sisters.

At age 12 her mother remarries; however, the constant reminders that her stepfather provides well for the family only fuels her dislike for him.

The sexual abuse starts soon after, almost always at the centre of DID diagnoses. An evil progression by her stepfather, from watching her shower and fondling lead to further ongoing abuse.

Desperate to protect her mother, Denise locked his secret away deep inside. Just two years later her stepfather's business partner, a 35-year-old man began abusing Denise creating further destruction to an already fragile mind. Along with the abuse came relentless crushing headaches, depression, and unusual lapses in time. Lapses, Denise later learnt, to be symptoms of the complex coping mechanism brought on by one of her alternate personalities taking over in an effort to share the load of her abuse.

After a spell of ill health and the removal of her right ovary and appendix, Denise was under diagnosed as suffering from post-operative depression. This led to an overdose of hay fever tablets, her first failed suicide attempt.

The crippling headaches continued. At night Denise screams into her pillow in pain and frustration. Finally, she breaks the silence turning to her mother for much needed support she tells of the abuse she has endured at the hands of her stepfather's business partner, still sparing her mother the details of her stepfather himself. Yet another devastating blow, instead of receiving the protection she so desires her mother simply asked her not to tell her stepfather as it would break his heart.

The ensuing three months are lost to Denise the stress once again causing one of the others to switch with her.

"I feel like I'm leading a double life", she says to a friend at 17, unaware that the numbers are far greater. Denise finally seeks the help of a councillor to deal with the constant black cloud of depression and heavy drops of guilt that rain down on her.

She looks back on her abuse with little emotion as though it happened to someone else, her body was there but her mind was not, someone else took the pain – Poppet or Mizzy or Quasi, still unbeknown to her – were there when she withdrew. So, without the emotion, what has she got to feel depressed about, the guilt continues to rain.

The councillor tells her a story of a young girl who loses her much loved father, who is abused, who feels alone and misunderstood. Through the rain, tears fall. By hearing her story as though it belongs to someone else, she feels the sadness in it.

Shifting in her chair now she tilts her head to the left, her eyes rise towards the ceiling. "They are all talking at once," she says, "the young ones are quietly saying 'tell her about us', some of the others are reminding me of things, saying tell her about this time or that."

Accustomed to blocking them out, she continues, recalling a reunion at age 25. Over dinner old friends laugh at stories of high school adventures. She is confused that they remember so many times that are lost to her and wonders why they all dwell on the past.

Amazingly Denise completes her education, works in management positions, marries twice, and raises her two children all the while suffering low self-esteem, depression, debilitating headaches and sometimes loosing days at a time. Both marriages fail as the pressure of her own life impedes on her relationships with those around her.

Eventually her working life is affected too. Work is completed without her remembering and exhaustion limits her working hours. Denise recalls with fear and embarrassment at a work function, her memories are clear, it was a Saturday night cruise on the Yarra, she was laughing, enjoying herself then she opens her eyes to see the familiar sight of her bedroom. It is Sunday afternoon. Frightened, she scrambles to find her jacket, handbag, any hints as to where the time had gone. Her purse is stuffed with money. Why?

Apprehensively, she faces her work mates on Monday only to be greeted with compliments. She had been the life of the party. In photos she sees the same person who occasionally takes her by surprise as she passes by a mirror, she was doing the limbo and had led the group to the casino where she wiped the blackjack table clean. Denise has never learnt the game.

Fifty years old and still looking for answers, Denise has been wrongly diagnosed and over medicated for literally a lifetime. Until she meets Annabel. Although the psychologist has limited experience with DID, after eight months she has confirmed her diagnoses.

She explains that the trauma of her father's death and the abuse she suffered caused her young mind to segregate different perceptions and emotions, these in turn generated different selves. Not all children who suffer abuse or trauma have the capacity to develop multiple personalities and those who do also have normal means of coping, if children who suffer abuse or trauma feel sufficiently protected and soothed by adults, Dissociative Identity Disorder does not develop.

For the diagnoses to be confirmed a person must display multiple distinct personalities, each with its own way of perceiving and interacting with the world. The diagnoses requires that at least two personalities routinely take control of the individual's behaviour with an associated memory loss that goes beyond normal forgetfulness.

DID is chronic, and it can be disabling even fatal although it is possible for some sufferers to function very well along with their alternate selves.

Overwhelmed with the diagnoses, Denise takes comfort within the safety of her home and the unconditional love of her canine companion, she doesn't leave for three months fearful of having no control over the emergence of her other selves. Finally, some relief sets in and her sessions with Annabel continue, gradually each of the personalities are revealed to Denise.

They each have names and Denise is able to visualize them as they speak to her or amongst themselves. She likens this to thinking of a friend, and as you do you are able to picture them clearly in your mind – this is the same for Denise and her alternate identities. As her ability to identify each personality evolves, she is able to pinpoint some of the switches and experience the emotions they felt at the time. Denise expresses this is the hardest part of the therapy.

Now when there are complete switches in personality there is still a loss of memory for that period, otherwise they go through life together – she may hear them all speaking at once or just a few. The mornings are hard, on waking they are all talking at once and each has their own agenda "lets feed the animals first, no we have to do the washing first, let's start work on the book". When someone asks her a question Denise may hear 12 other responses, not all in agreement which can sometimes bring about panic. She often forgets to eat due to the constant distractions and relies heavily on her ever-mounting to do lists.

When mental exhaustion creeps in, Denise can block out the voices by concentrating on a computer game, threatening to take the prescribed 1mg of Xanax and, when necessary, does so. Clinical depression co-exists with the DID requiring antidepressants, and her headaches caused by the brain switches from one personality to another are relieved with prescription analgesics.

After coming to terms with DID, Denise reveals her condition to her family, painfully they turn away from her. Her mother seems not to understand, and her sisters ignore it in hope the condition may simply disappear.

On September 11, 2001 Denise has made the difficult decision to unlock her secret and tell her mother about the abuse she was exposed to by her stepfather. Initially, her mother shows concern and asks why she never told her.

"Because I thought I was protecting you", she replies.

Confronting David as a family, her mother asks if he knows what they might be about to ask him. In a near admission of guilt he says he has a fair idea. His full admission comes with the words "she enjoyed it". Her mother stands by his side and ceases contact.

To her friends the diagnoses explains so much. They now realise what they had believed to be mood swings were in fact meetings with her alters. To her children the news comes with tears of relief, grateful to finally have much needed answers. They can now recognise and interact with the more prominent personalities. Poppet was the first to emerge, she is young and loves children. Mizzy is a wild teenager who desperately wants to fit in while Janice is nice, she can also be the truly angry one.

Denise has taken up bee keeping for Jon who loves animals. Quasi is blue and beaten from taking most of the abuse for Denise. Then there is Marm; she is tidy and regimented.

Integration is a common treatment process, one that Denise feels is not necessary now that her selves can cooperate sufficiently. "Prior to my diagnoses I was lost, lonely and confused but didn't know it, while DID can be exhausting and isolating it can also be enjoyable and I feel I am one of the luckiest people alive."

She believes the course her life has taken has happened for a reason and as her autobiography nears publication, she hopes it will bring her life new meaning. Her main goal is to raise awareness, acceptance and create questions – questions she hopes to answer as a lecturer, her next goal.

ABOUT THE AUTHOR

Many years passed before Denise Grant was given her diagnoses of Dissociative Identity Disorder. It was only with the benefit of hindsight that she began to realise that the many blank periods of her life began to make sense. Until her late-forties, she had been labelled as Clinically Depressed. To say her life had been a roller coaster ride, was an understatement.

She developed the ability to observe scenes from her life as though they were happening to someone else. It was a truly remarkable survival technique and she counts herself as one of the luckiest people alive as this disorder is associated with horrid flashbacks, suicidal thoughts, mood swings, memory loss, panic attacks, and depression.

Formerly known as multiple personalities, Dissociative Identity Disorder helped Denise Grant to function and navigate her way through a very colourful life. The eldest of three sisters, she experienced emotional neglect as a child, the early death of her father when she was ten years old, and sexual abuse by her stepfather and others during her early teens. She counts herself incredibly lucky as the use of other methods to ease the pain such as suicide, alcoholism and drug addiction were avoided. She is passionate about removing stigma surrounding mental health issues. She has been involved with a major organisation speaking out publicly about her personal experiences to educate and bring hope to many.

ACKNOWLEDGEMENTS

So many to thank so where do I start.

My daughter, Jodie and my son, Corey would be a good start. They have dealt with so much due to having me as a Mum. It has not always been easy for them, and I would like to take this time to say a big "Thank You" to both of them.

My special friends, Ray and Carmel. Although I must have led them on a merry dance with much confusion in tow, they have stuck by me all this time and I am so grateful to them both.

Annabel. After many, she was the only psychologist, who saw something about me that no one else had ever noticed before. My book started as journals I wrote each week for her, and with lots of patience and much jocularity she helped me to make sense of my topsy turvy life.

My present professional support team Melanie, Christina and Aimee are always there for me and seem to be able to put things in a such a way that brings me back to the "Real World."

My psychiatrist is also a valued support person for me, and he treats me with much respect as he acknowledges the good and bad times that are part and parcel of my colourful life.

Julie, my mentor has helped me so much in bringing this book to life. Her encouragement and faith in me, which at times must have been daunting, has never allowed me give up.

Charlotte. A talented wordsmith who was able to cleverly make sense of all my journals in a sensitive and insightful way.

Amanda. Her professional skills as an editor has been invaluable and I appreciate the help she has given me with the final editing of my book.

Sophie, my book designer. She turned my book into a work of art.

There have been many others, but to be able to thank them all, I would probably have to write another book.

Life is like a book.
Some chapters sad, some
happy and some exciting.
But if you never turn the page.
You will never know what
the next chapter holds.

~e.buddhism.com

www.ingramcontent.com/pod-product-compliance
Lightning Source LLC
Chambersburg PA
CBHW021908020426
42334CB00013B/514

* 9 780648 697909 *